AUGMENTATIVE AND ALTERNATIVE COMMUNICATION FOR ADULTS WITH APHASIA

AUGMENTATIVE AND ALTERNATIVE
COMMUNICATIONS PERSPECTIVES   VOLUME 3

AUGMENTATIVE AND ALTERNATIVE COMMUNICATION FOR ADULTS WITH APHASIA

EDITED BY

RAJINDER KOUL

*Department of Speech, Language and Hearing Sciences,
Texas Tech University Health Sciences Center,
Lubbock, Texas*

Emerald

United Kingdom – North America – Japan
India – Malaysia – China

Emerald Group Publishing Limited
Howard House, Wagon Lane, Bingley BD16 1WA, UK

First edition 2011

British Library Cataloguing in Publication Data
A catalogue record for this book is available from the British Library

ISBN: 978-1-84855-218-0
ISSN: 2047-0991 (Series)

Emerald Group Publishing
Limited, Howard House,
Environmental Management
System has been certified by
ISOQAR to ISO 14001:2004
standards

Awarded in recognition of
Emerald's production
department's adherence to
quality systems and processes
when preparing scholarly
journals for print

INVESTOR IN PEOPLE

CONTENTS

CHAPTER 5   EFFICACY OF NO-TECHNOLOGY-BASED AAC INTERVENTION APPROACHES   *79*
Melinda Corwin

CHAPTER 6   AAC AND MESSAGE ENHANCEMENT FOR PERSONS WITH APHASIA   *93*
Ann R. Beck

LIST OF CONTRIBUTORS

Ann R. Beck   Department of Communication Sciences
                       and Disorders, Illinois State University,
                       Normal, IL, USA

Melinda Corwin   Department of Speech, Language and
                       Hearing Sciences, Texas Tech University
                       Health Sciences Center, Lubbock,
                       TX, USA

Rajinder Koul   Department of Speech, Language and
                       Hearing Sciences, Texas Tech University
                       Health Sciences Center, Lubbock, TX,
                       USA

Nidhi Mahendra   Department of Communicative Sciences
                       and Disorders, California State University
                       East Bay, Hayward, CA, USA

Ralf W. Schlosser   Speech-Language Pathology & Audiology,
                       School Psychology Program, Counseling &
                       Applied Educational Psychology,
                       Northeastern University, Boston, MA,
                       USA, and Center for Communication
                       Enhancement, Children's Hospital Boston,
                       Boston, MA, USA

SERIES FOREWORD

The *Augmentative and Alternative Communication (AAC) Perspectives Series* is an opened-ended series of small to moderately sized books focusing on specific topics within the field of AAC. These extensively referenced books are based on the three cornerstones of evidence-based practice (EBP): research, clinical and/or educational expertise, and stakeholders' perspectives. They are designed to serve as (1) primary texts for courses with an emphasis on AAC, (2) supplemental texts for broad-based courses in AAC, and (3) professional resources for researchers and practicing clinicians/educators.

The series is designed to help fill the need for texts that relate basic principles and new developments in AAC to specific topics in communication disorders and special education. The first book of the series focuses on an emerging area that had received attention in the AAC literature but had not yet been treated comprehensively in a text. This inaugural book of the series, *The Efficacy of Augmentative and Alternative Communication: Toward Evidenced-Based Practice* (Schlosser, 2003), was the first book in both communication disorders and special education to address the critical aspects of efficacy and EBP.

The second book in the series, *Literacy and Augmentative and Alternative Communication* (Smith, 2005), deals with the development of literacy in individuals with severe disabilities and little or no functional speech. Numerous refereed journal articles and book chapters had been written about literacy and AAC, but no text had yet been published. Smith covers the subject of literacy and AAC in great depth providing clear information and engaging discussion on general models of literacy acquisition, principals of literacy assessment and intervention, and the use of specific approaches and technologies as they relate to AAC users.

Augmentative and Alternative Communication for Adults with Aphasia by Rajinder K. Koul, is the first book on aphasia with extensive coverage of AAC. The book provides an overview of aphasia as well as a comprehensive review of AAC interventions. Koul examines intervention strategies and techniques. He provides insightful discussion about primary and secondary stakeholders' feelings about the effectiveness of AAC interventions. The book is designed to be a resource for users of AAC and their families; students in professional preparation programs; service providers including occupational therapists, physical therapists, special educators, speech-language pathologists; and applied researchers.

Koul has distinguished himself as a leader in the field of AAC. He is currently a professor and department chair at Texas Tech University Health Science Center and associate dean for Research for the School of Allied Health Sciences. Koul has an impressive list of publications on aphasia in professional journals and has authored several book chapters. Publications that are most relevant to this book include "Comparison of Graphic Symbol Learning in Individuals with Aphasia and Right Hemisphere Brain Damage" (Koul & Lloyd, 1998), "Production of Graphic Symbol Sentences by Individuals with Aphasia: Efficacy of a Computer-Based Augmentative and Alternative Communication Intervention" (Koul, Corwin, & Hayes, 2005), "Training Individuals with Severe Broca's Aphasia To Produce Sentences Using Graphic Symbols: Implications for AAC Intervention" (Koul, Corwin, Nigam, & Oetzel, 2008), and "Systematic Review of Speech Generating Devices for Aphasia" (Koul, Petroi, & Schlosser, 2010). Koul's leadership has been recognized in many ways. For example, he was the recipient of the Mary E. Switzer Distinguished Rehabilitation Research Fellowship from the National Institute on Disability and Rehabilitation Research in 2002 and was named a Fellow of the American Speech, Language and Hearing Association (ASHA) in 2005.

Augmentative and Alternative Communication for Adults with Aphasia provides a wealth of synthesized information that translates research into practice. The book is expected to be a valuable resource that can serve as a text in courses on aphasia and as a reference for stakeholders in the intervention process. Additional books in the series will focus on topics that have been discussed in journals and book chapters but that still show a need for more extensive discussion on the perspectives of AAC. Some of the books in the series will emphasize research and basic information. Others will emphasize clinical and educational practice. All the books will relate to aspects of the broad communication model originally proposed by Lloyd, Quist, and Windsor (1990) and subsequently discussed in later publications (e.g., Fuller & Lloyd, 1997).

Lyle L. Lloyd
Series Editor
Helen H. Arvidson
Associate Editor

REFERENCES

Fuller, D. R., & Lloyd, L. L. (1997). AAC model and taxonomy. In: L. L. Lloyd, D. R. Fuller & H. H. Arvidson (Eds), *Augmentative and alternative communication: A handbook of principles and practices* (pp. 25–37). Boston, MA: Allyn and Bacon.

Koul, R. K., Corwin, M., & Hayes, S. (2005). Production of graphic symbol sentences by individuals with aphasia: Efficacy of a computer-based augmentative and alternative communication intervention. *Brain and Language, 92*, 58–77.

Koul, R. K., Corwin, M., Nigam, R., & Oetzel, S. (2008). Training individuals with severe Broca's aphasia to produce sentences using graphic symbols: Implications for AAC intervention. *Journal of Assistive Technologies, 2*, 23–34.

Koul, R. K., & Lloyd, L. L. (1998). Comparison of graphic symbol learning in individuals with aphasia and right hemisphere brain damage. *Brain and Language, 62*, 398–421.

Koul, R. K., Petroi, D., & Schlosser, R. (2010). Systematic review of speech generating devices for aphasia. In: S. Stern & J. W. Mullennix (Eds), *Computer synthesized speech technologies: Tools for aiding impairment* (pp. 148–160). Hershey, PA: IGI Global.

Lloyd, L. L., Quist, R. W., & Windsor, J. (1990). A proposed augmentative and alternative communication model. *Augmentatives and Alternative Communication, 6*, 172–183.

Schlosser, R. W. (2003). *The efficacy of augmentative and alternative communication.* San Diego, CA: Academic Press.

Smith, M. M. (2005). *Literacy and augmentative and alternative communication.* San Diego, CA: Elsevier Academic Press.

In memory of my father (Jawahar Lal Koul)
and
for my mother (Jai Kishori Koul)
and
To Rubini, my wife and best friend

ACKNOWLEDGMENTS

I am grateful to Jessica E. Lierly and Helen H. Arvidson for reviewing the manuscript. Their suggestions have helped me improve the quality of the manuscript. I also express my special appreciation to graduate students and faculty colleagues in the Department of Speech, Language, and Hearing Sciences at Texas Tech University Health Sciences Center who over the years have directly or indirectly contributed to much of my work in the area of augmentative and alternative communication (AAC) and aphasia. I also appreciate the encouragement from Lyle L. Lloyd and Ralf W. Schlosser, who talked me into producing this book. Finally, I thank the many people with aphasia who have participated in AAC intervention studies across the world. Without their support, this book would not have been possible.

FOREWORD

It is both a pleasure and an honor to be asked to write this foreword for *Augmentative and Alternative Communication for Adults with Aphasia.* Aphasia is one of several acquired neurologic disorders that can lead to candidacy for augmentative and alternative communication (AAC) interventions. Thus far, we have seen individual chapters on this topic (e.g., Garrett & Kimelman, 2000; Garrett & Lasker, 2005; Koul & Corwin, 2003) in books that cover AAC with a broader range of acquired disorders or books that aim to be introductory texts to AAC. Until now there has not been a focused effort to synthesize what we know into a single cohesive book. Yet, the evidence base for AAC interventions in aphasia has grown over the years, and the timing is excellent to take stock of where the field is and where it needs go.

I cannot think of anyone who is more qualified to write this book than Dr. Rajinder Koul. Not only is he a certified clinician with practical experiences with this population, but he has also contributed to the research base in this area through data-based articles in peer-reviewed journals. His publications span such prestigious journals as the *Journal of Speech, Language and Hearing Research* to *Brain and Language* to *Augmentative and Alternative Communication.*

Although there are many scientific studies one could discuss, I would like to highlight his article in the 2005 volume of *Brain and Language*, entitled "Production of graphic symbol sentences by individuals with aphasia: Efficacy of a computer-based augmentative and alternative communication intervention" (Koul, Corwin, & Hayes, 2005). What is remarkable about this study is not so much that it is published in a prestigious journal. It is rather that this study involved *nine individuals* with aphasia who were tested for their ability to produce graphic symbol sentences of varying syntactical complexity using a software program that turns a computer into a speech generating device. In the world of single-subject experimental research, nine replications are rare, to say the least. It is this kind of research that will elevate AAC research with individuals with aphasia into the realm of high quality empirically supported interventions that is so essential to evidence-based practice. This article was ranked among the top 25 articles published in *Brain and Language* at the time of the publication. Dr. Koul has also been active on various editorial boards including *Augmentative and Alternative Communication, Evidence-Based Communication Assessment and Intervention*, and *Journal of Speech, Language, and Hearing Research*. He has been named a fellow of the American Speech-Language and Hearing Association, indicating his excellent standing in the field.

Thus, without doubt Dr. Koul has the expertise to critically engage with the evidence base and draw appropriate conclusions, and issue calls for future research. To supplement his own writing, Dr. Koul has invited several contributors who are known for their area of expertise, including Drs. Ann Beck, Melinda Corwin, Nidhi Mahendra, and myself. This book continues the tradition set forth in earlier contributions to the AAC book series with its focus on translating research to practice and moving the field closer to evidence-based practice. I am confident that this groundbreaking book will stimulate future research with this important population.

Ralf W. Schlosser

REFERENCES

Garrett, K. L., & Kimelman, M. D. Z. (2000). AAC and aphasia: Cognitive-linguistic considerations. In: D. R. Beukelman, K. M. Yorkston & J. Reichle (Eds), *Augmentative and alternative communication for adults with acquired neurologic disorders* (pp. 339–374). Baltimore, MD: Paul H. Brookes Publishing Company.

Garrett, K. L., & Lasker, J. P. (2005). Adults with severe aphasia. In: D. R. Beukelman & P. Mirenda (Eds), *Augmentative and alternative communication: Supporting children and adults with complex communication needs* (3rd ed., pp. 467–504). Baltimore, MD: Paul H. Brookes.

Koul, R., & Corwin, M. (2003). Efficacy of AAC intervention in individuals with chronic severe aphasia. In: R. W. Schlosser (Ed.), *The efficacy of augmentative and alternative communication: Toward evidence-based practice* (pp. 449–471). San Diego, CA: Academic Press.

Koul, R., Corwin, M., & Hayes, S. (2005). Production of graphic symbol sentences by individuals with aphasia: Efficacy of a computer-based augmentative and alternative communication intervention. *Brain and Language, 92*, 58–77.

CHAPTER 1

INTRODUCTION

Rajinder Koul

INTRODUCTION

Augmentative and Alternative Communication (AAC) for Adults with Aphasia is a text written for practicing clinicians, undergraduate and graduate students, assistive technologists, and other stakeholders who are interested in learning more about the communication needs and options for people with aphasia. Although there are several book chapters dedicated to aphasia in currently available textbooks in AAC, this is the first book dedicated entirely to AAC and aphasia. Aphasia is a language impairment resulting from damage to areas of the brain that are responsible for interpretation and formulation of language. The most common cause of aphasia is a stroke. Persons with aphasia may demonstrate deficits in any one, multiple, or all major areas of language function: spontaneous speech, comprehension, reading, and writing. Data on incidence of aphasia and stroke indicates that about 66 per 100,000 people in the United Kingdom have aphasia (Enderby & Emerson, 1995), and approximately 100,000 people acquire aphasia every year in the United States (National Aphasia Association, 2011). Although the incident rates for strokes across the world vary somewhat, several studies indicate that in most areas about 300 per 100,000 to 500 per 100,000 people acquire stroke-related brain injury per year (Sudlow & Warlow, 1997). Furthermore, the prevalence of aphasia across the world will increase in the future as the proportion of populations above 65 years of age grows. About two-thirds of all strokes occur in people

Augmentative and Alternative Communication for Adults with Aphasia
Augmentative and Alternative Communications Perspectives, Volume 3, 1–5
Copyright © 2011 by Emerald Group Publishing Limited
All rights of reproduction in any form reserved
ISSN: 2047-0991/doi:10.1108/S2047-0991(2011)0000003007

over 65 years of age in the United States (Centers for Disease Control and Prevention, 2011). Thus, it is important that practicing clinicians and pre-professional students have the resources that will allow them to gain both knowledge and skills to make informed decisions related to provision of AAC services to persons with aphasia. In preparing this book, I had the following objectives:

- To provide an overview of aphasia and various treatment approaches.
- To provide a comprehensive review of AAC intervention approaches for persons with aphasia.
- To evaluate the efficacy of AAC intervention approaches that use technology, such as speech generating devices, and non-technological AAC approaches as part of a treatment package.
- To examine the ways in which AAC techniques and strategies can be applied to persons with aphasia.
- To better understand how both direct stakeholders (i.e., persons with aphasia) and indirect stakeholders (e.g., close and extended family members, friends, paid caregivers) feel about the effectiveness of AAC intervention in persons with aphasia.

OVERVIEW OF INDIVIDUAL CHAPTERS

The second chapter of the book, *Overview of Aphasia and Approaches to Aphasia Intervention*, by Nidhi Mahendra, provides the reader with an introduction to aphasia and associated disorders. This chapter also focuses on various subtypes of aphasia and on communication intervention approaches that are used to treat persons with aphasia. Nidhi Mahendra uses the World Health Organization's International Classification of Functioning, Disability, and Health (World Health Organization, 2001) in conceptualizing the diverse intervention approaches available in clinical armamentarium.

Chapter 3, *Overview of AAC Intervention Approaches for Persons with Aphasia*, by Rajinder Koul, introduces the reader to various AAC options available to persons with aphasia. This chapter includes (1) technologically based and non-technological AAC intervention options and (2) AAC intervention approaches based on communication needs, competencies, and participation levels. The strength of this chapter is that examples presented clearly elucidate the availability of a range of AAC options for persons with aphasia.

Chapter 4, *Efficacy of Technologically Based AAC Intervention Approaches*, by Rajinder Koul, is a systematic review of AAC intervention studies that involved technology as one of the components of an AAC intervention treatment package. This chapter (1) describes the characteristics of the participants, (2) evaluates intervention outcomes, and (3) appraises the methodological quality of studies. Evaluating the efficacy of AAC intervention approaches is critical because funding agencies are increasingly demanding empirical data that can be used to support the use of assistive technologies such as speech generating devices in persons with severe communication impairments.

Melinda Corwin's Chapter 5, *Efficacy of No-Technology-Based AAC Intervention Approaches*, provides a review of various unaided and aided AAC strategies including partner-dependent approaches to AAC intervention. This chapter primarily focuses on no-technology techniques and strategies that clinicians can use to facilitate communication in persons with aphasia. The author also discusses the state of AAC efficacy research in the context of the prevailing theoretical conceptualization of clinical efficacy and outcome research.

Chapter 6, *AAC and Message Enhancement for Persons with Aphasia*, by Ann R. Beck, focuses on the importance of vocabulary organization, message display, and rate enhancement in AAC intervention for persons with aphasia. Beck reviews several studies on AAC intervention in persons with aphasia and draws implications for message enhancement that should be of interest to practicing clinicians. The work reviewed in this chapter is directly relevant to the development and design of technologies that may potentially help persons with aphasia become effective and efficient communicators.

Ralf W. Schlosser in Chapter 7, *What Do Social Validation Data Tell Us about AAC Interventions?* introduces the reader to the importance of social validation in AAC intervention research. Specifically, this chapter defines social validation and its methods and provides an AAC social validity framework. It is important that AAC interventions be considered socially valid by both direct and indirect stakeholders in order for those interventions to be carried out successfully in day-to-day functional communicative situations.

Chapter 8, *Social Validation of Augmentative and Alternative Communication Interventions in Aphasia* written by Melinda Corwin, reviews studies that have evaluated social validation of AAC interventions in persons with aphasia. She provides case examples that elucidate various quantitative and qualitative measures that are used to assess social validity of interventions.

Chapter 9, *The Process of Evidence-Based Practice: Informing AAC Clinical Decisions for Persons with Aphasia* written by Rajinder Koul and Melinda Corwin, is the concluding chapter that examines available data on the efficacy of AAC intervention for persons with aphasia using an evidence-based practice process. The integration of the best research evidence with clinical expertise and perspectives of stakeholders is the key to bridging the gap between research and clinical practice.

WHO WILL THIS BOOK BENEFIT?

This book is geared toward students, practitioners, researchers, and educators who are interested in the areas of AAC and aphasia. Specifically, this book will be of interest to speech-language pathologists, rehabilitation scientists and engineers, psychologists, neurologists, and assistive technologists. The book's primary emphasis is on providing information to current and future clinical practitioners so that they can make informed decisions about using AAC with persons with aphasia. Additionally, this book is an attempt to bridge the gap between research and clinical practice. With the advent of evidence-based practice in health care, it has become critical to evaluate the available evidence on the efficacy of AAC intervention in persons with aphasia. It is my hope that this book will inspire both clinicians and researchers to develop and evaluate AAC intervention strategies and techniques that are oriented towards facilitating communication in persons with aphasia.

CONCLUSION

In the past two decades, significant clinical advances have been made in developing and implementing AAC assessment and intervention strategies in persons with aphasia who have severe communication limitations. This book comprehensively reviews those advances and identifies critical gaps that must be filled in order for AAC interventions to become an essential part of clinical armamentarium in rehabilitation of persons with aphasia.

REFERENCES

Centers for Disease Control and Prevention. (2011). *Stroke facts.* Retrieved from http://www.cdc.gov/stroke/facts.htm

Enderby, P., & Emerson, J. (1995). Speech and language therapy: Does it work? *British Medical Journal, 312,* 1655.

National Aphasia Association. (2011). *Aphasia frequently asked questions.* Retrieved from http://www.aphasia.org/Aphasia%20Facts/aphasia_faq.html

Sudlow, C. L., & Warlow, C. P. (1997). Comparable studies of the incidence of stroke and its pathological types. *Stroke, 28,* 491–499.

World Health Organization. (2011). *World Health Organization.* Retrieved from http://www.who.int/en/

CHAPTER 2

OVERVIEW OF APHASIA AND APPROACHES TO APHASIA INTERVENTION

Nidhi Mahendra

INTRODUCTION

Aphasia is an acquired neurogenic language disorder characterized by impairment of an individual's ability to comprehend and produce language symbols for everyday communication. Aphasia is the most common communication disorder resulting from brain damage. Cerebrovascular accidents (CVAs) or strokes are the leading cause of aphasia in adults. However, aphasia also may result from brain trauma, brain tumors, or a specific inflammatory or neurodegenerative disease process.

INCIDENCE AND PREVALENCE

According to the National Stroke Association (NSA) (2006), stroke is the third leading cause of death in the United States (after heart disease and cancer) and is the leading cause of disability in adults. Further, the NSA reports that approximately 5.4 million Americans are living with the effects of stroke at any given time. Recent epidemiological data provided by the American Heart Association (AHA, 2003) reveal that nearly 700,000

Augmentative and Alternative Communication for Adults with Aphasia
Augmentative and Alternative Communications Perspectives, Volume 3, 7–46
Copyright © 2011 by Emerald Group Publishing Limited
ISSN: 2047-0991/doi:10.1108/S2047-0991(2011)0000003008

individuals in the United States experience a new or recurring stroke each year, and the reported incidence of stroke is on the rise (Williams, Jiang, Matchar, & Samsa, 1999). Two-thirds of the individuals who experience a stroke survive and require post-stroke rehabilitation (National Institute of Neurological Disorders and Stroke, 2002). An estimated one million individuals in the United States currently have aphasia (National Institute on Deafness and Other Communication Disorders, 2006).

DOMAINS AFFECTED AS A RESULT OF APHASIA

Depending on the site and extent of the neuroanatomical lesion resulting from a CVA or other brain damage, aphasia results in language impairments affecting spoken and written modalities including word retrieval (naming), fluency, auditory comprehension, repetition, reading comprehension, and written language production. According to Davis (2007), aphasia selectively impairs the cognitive systems and processes necessary for the comprehension and use of language, and therefore, may be regarded as a cognitive impairment. Additionally, several researchers have demonstrated that aphasia impairs select processes in cognitive domains, such as attention (Murray, 2002; Laures, Odell, & Coe, 2003), working memory (Wright, Newhoff, Downey, & Austermann, 2003; Wright & Shisler, 2005), verbal episodic memory (Beeson, Bayles, Rubens, & Kaszniak, 1993), spatial memory (Burgio & Basso, 1997), and executive function (Mayer, Murray, Turkstra, & Lorenzen, 2006).

DISORDERS ACCOMPANYING APHASIA

Aphasia is frequently associated with concomitant disorders affecting motor speech functions (e.g., dysarthria or apraxia of speech), sensory recognition (agnosia), reading (alexia), writing (agraphia), and swallowing ability (dysphagia). These disorders are discussed briefly below.

Dysarthria

Dysarthria (*Greek: dys = damaged + arthron = articulation*) is a collective term for a group of neurogenic speech disorders resulting from impairment of the neuromuscular execution of speech (Duffy, 2005). Dysarthria may be associated with damage to single or multiple sites along the motor pathway from the cerebral cortex to the muscles involved in speech production. Specifically, dysarthria may result from damage to the upper motor neuron system, lower motor neuron system, extrapyramidal system, the cerebellum, basal ganglia, or a combination of these areas. Dysarthria may involve any or all subcomponents of the speech production system – respiration, phonation, articulation, resonance, and prosody.

Apraxia

Apraxia (*Greek: a = without + praxis = action*) is a neurogenic speech disorder characterized by impaired "capacity to plan or program sensorimotor commands necessary for directing movements that result in phonetically and prosodically normal speech" (Duffy, 2005, p. 307). Apraxia occurs in the absence of paralysis, paresis, or evidence of muscular weakness. In other words, the term apraxia denotes an individual's inability to carry out skilled motor actions on volition, especially when the person understands the task, and is able to carry out the required motor command in a different context. For example, an individual may be unable to touch his face with both hands when asked to do so, but has no difficulty touching his cheeks with his hands to apply aftershave lotion.

Apraxia may be divided into two types – ideomotor and ideational. Ideomotor apraxia is characterized by difficulty in the sequencing and execution of movements such that an affected individual is unable to correctly sequence a series of movements to achieve a desired action (e.g., when asked "Show me how you put butter on your toast"). Ideational apraxia is characterized by an individual's inability to perform a series of acts with the preserved ability to perform the individual components of the series. For instance, brushing one's teeth requires squeezing toothpaste out of a tube onto a toothbrush, followed by using the toothbrush to brush teeth, and then washing the toothbrush clean. An individual with ideational apraxia may be able to perform each of these steps correctly but in an incorrect sequence. This type of apraxia is thought to result from the loss of conceptual knowledge associated with object use and the overall purpose of the activity sequence.

Apraxias may be of different types, depending on the specific type of skilled motor movement or activity that is impaired. For instance, individuals may present with apraxia of speech (AOS), limb or buccofacial apraxia, constructional apraxia, dressing apraxia, etc. AOS is a motor speech disorder that results in an impaired ability to program speech muscles and sequence muscle movements for the volitional production of phonemes and words, necessary for speech (Darley, Aronson, & Brown, 1975). It is noteworthy that AOS is not associated with neuromuscular impairments secondary to paralysis, motor incoordination, or sensory deficits. AOS has been associated with lesions to Broca's area, the insula (Dronkers, 1996), and left frontal and/or parietal cortices, as well as left subcortical areas (Miller, 2002).

Agnosia

Brookshire (2007) describes *agnosia* (*Greek: a = without + gnosis = knowledge*) as a generic term for an inability to recognize sensory stimuli (e.g., an object or a picture) in the absence of perceptual deficits involving the specific modality (hearing, touch, or vision). Agnosia may be auditory, visual, or tactile in nature.

Agraphia

Agraphia (*Greek: a = without + graphein = to write*) is an acquired writing disorder in which the ability to write and spell (i.e., to produce graphemes) is impaired subsequent to a stroke or other brain damage. Agraphia can be divided into lexical (or surface agraphia) and phonological types. In lexical agraphia, an individual presents with impaired spelling characterized by "over-reliance on sound-to-letter conversions" (Klein & Mancinelli, 2010, p. 102). Individuals with lexical agraphia have no difficulty spelling words with conventional sound-to-letter correspondence (e.g., mat) but are impaired at spelling irregular words (e.g., circuit, which may be misspelled as *surkit or sirkit*). In phonological agraphia, affected individuals can write common words (including irregularly spelled words) but cannot spell nonwords (e.g., *mofer*). Beeson, Antonucci, Henry, & White (2004) have reported that lexical agraphia is caused by left extrasylvian lesions resulting in impairment at the level of orthographic word forms. This is contrasted with phonological agraphia which results from left perisylvian cortical lesions that result in impaired phonological processing (Beeson, Rising, Kim, & Rapcsak, 2010).

Alexia

Beeson and Hillis (2001) define *alexia* as an acquired inability to recognize strings of letters as familiar words, despite no impairment in the ability to perceive individual letters. Alexia may accompany agraphia or occur in a pure form without agraphia (also called posterior or occipital alexia). When an individual presents with pure alexia (i.e., alexia without agraphia), the ability to write words spontaneously or to dictation remains preserved but reading processes are specifically impaired. Individuals with pure alexia usually can comprehend words that are spelled out aloud suggesting that their spelling abilities are spared. One of the striking patterns of performance seen in an individual with pure alexia is that he/she may write a sentence or phrase and then be completely unable to read what has been written. Kiran (2006) describes pure alexia as a reading disorder in which an individual has a specific deficit in the initial stages of visual processing of written words. Persons with pure alexia have difficulty visually analyzing the features of written stimuli as well as recognizing written stimuli as familiar, with input from the visual lexicon. Most often, alexia without agraphia results from a stroke in the region of distribution of the left posterior cerebral artery (PCA).

In alexia with agraphia (also called central or parietal alexia), the site of lesion is likely to be the inferior parietal lobule, comprising the angular and supramarginal gyri. An individual who has alexia with agraphia presents with a near total reading disorder and limited writing ability. Unlike individuals with pure alexia, persons presenting with alexia and agraphia are unable to comprehend words that are spelled aloud and often cannot copy letters.

Dysphagia

Dysphagia is defined as "an impaired ability to move food or liquid from the mouth to the stomach" (Logemann, 1997, p. 1) and is common in individuals post-stroke. Based on a recent review of the literature conducted by Martino et. al. (2005), estimates of the incidence of dysphagia in stroke patients vary, depending on the assessment procedure used, from approximately 37–45% (based on cursory screening for dysphagia) to 51–55% (based on using clinical bedside examination) to as high as 64–78% (based on using instrumental assessment such as the modified barium swallow).

DIFFERENTIAL DIAGNOSIS

Aphasia versus Right Hemisphere Damage

Aphasia can be differentiated from right hemisphere damage (RHD) based on the presence and type of communicative impairments, as well as other concomitant cognitive deficits. First, not all patients with RHD have communication impairments (Brookshire, 2007) and when present, these impairments differ markedly from aphasia (Myers, 2001). Most patients with RHD function fairly adequately on a superficial communicative level but experience difficulty in complex and more abstract communicative situations. Often the communicative impairments in RHD accompany associated deficits in perceptual processing (e.g., neglect, agnosia, visuospatial perception impairments, etc.), affect and emotion regulation, discourse cohesion and coherence, interpreting figurative language, and extralinguistic cues (e.g., tone of voice or facial expressions), and pragmatic aspects of communication such as turn-taking and topic maintenance during conversation (Myers, 2001). Further, RHD is associated with specific cognitive deficits impacting attention (e.g., resulting in neglect as well as sustained and divided attention impairments), orientation, memory (e.g., especially working memory and visuospatial memory), executive function (e.g., decision making, problem-solving, planning, and self-awareness of deficits), and impulse control.

Aphasia versus Dementia

Grabowski and Damasio (2004, p. 2) define dementia as "an acquired and persistent impairment of intellectual faculties, affecting several cognitive domains, that is sufficiently severe to impair competence in daily living, occupation, and social interaction." Dementias may be reversible or irreversible in nature. Aphasia can be differentially diagnosed from irreversible dementias (e.g., Alzheimer's disease) based on: (1) a careful case history and establishing the nature of symptom onset (gradual versus acute), (2) analysis of the symptoms present (memory deficits and anomia are often the earliest noted problems in dementia whereas aphasia is characterized by significant impairments in fluency, auditory comprehension, motor speech production, or reading comprehension), (3) presence of any unilateral paralysis of limb and/or oromotor muscles, and (4) detailed study of findings from structural brain imaging scans.

Differentially diagnosing aphasia from reversible dementias (e.g., dementia-like symptoms resulting from normal pressure hydrocephalus, depression or pseudodementia, or acute renal insufficiency) requires careful review of the patient's medical chart, prior medical history, and pattern of onset of current symptoms. A detailed medical work-up (including blood work, an electrolyte panel, CT and/or structural MRI scans, etc.) will usually reveal an alternative explanation for the patient's symptoms (e.g., raised intracranial pressure, abnormal thyroid function, adverse drug interactions, etc.). Finally, a quick and marked improvement in a patient's symptoms after a medical course of treatment usually points to a reversible dementia, not aphasia.

Aphasia versus Traumatic Brain Injury

Persons with traumatic brain injury (TBI) almost always sustain injury to the prefrontal cortex as well as to frontal lobe regions anterior to the primary and supplementary motor cortices (Hartley, 1995). When compared with individuals who have aphasia secondary to a left hemisphere CVA, this damage to the frontal and prefrontal cortices results in persons with TBI being much more likely to present with cognitive and metacognitive problems such as post-traumatic amnesia, episodic and working memory impairments, executive function deficits, reduced self-awareness of impairments, and low motivation and drive to participate in intervention. Persons with TBI also frequently present with challenging behaviors, such as extreme disinhibition, impulsivity, aggression, impatience, and irritability. Finally, persons with TBI typically present with a history of an event or activity resulting in a direct closed head or open head (penetrating) injury. Aphasia is mostly caused by CVAs, which are regarded as a nontraumatic type of brain injury.

TYPES OF APHASIA SYNDROMES

Classifying an individual's language impairment as a distinct type of aphasia is useful because it facilitates communication between clinicians and/or members of the interdisciplinary team about spared and impaired abilities as well as about a performance profile across varied language tasks. Further, classifying the type of aphasia may offer some insight into a potential neuroanatomical site of lesion. The aphasia syndromes are best understood as broad phenotypes that may accompany different types of brain damage. There are multiple ways to classify types of aphasia; some more widely used than others. The most commonly used classification systems (Haynes & Pindzola, 2004) are fluent versus nonfluent aphasia, perisylvian versus extrasylvian aphasias (Benson & Ardila, 1996), the "Boston" classification which is based on a client's test performance on the Boston Diagnostic Aphasia Examination (BDAE) (Goodglass, Kaplan, & Barresi, 2001), and the Western Aphasia Battery-Revised (WAB-R) classification (Kertesz, 2007).

Fluent versus Nonfluent Aphasia

One important dimension that is clinically used to classify aphasia is whether the nature and amount of spontaneous verbal production is relatively fluent or nonfluent (Goodglass & Kaplan, 1972). Individuals with fluent aphasia typically are better able to produce propositional sentences with preserved syntax, phonology, and prosody (Kertesz, 2007). These individuals demonstrate word-finding errors, paraphasias, circumlocution, and jargon. On the contrary, individuals with nonfluent aphasia are unable to speak in complete sentences. These individuals may be nonverbal or may produce telegraphic speech, recurrent stereotypic utterances, paraphasias, severe word finding difficulty, hesitations, and altered phonology and prosody. Generally speaking, damage to anterior lesions is associated with nonfluent aphasias, whereas damage to posterior lesions results in fluent aphasias.

Perisylvian versus Extrasylvian Aphasia

This classification is based on whether an aphasia-causing lesion is located in the critical language areas located around the Sylvian fissure (therefore, perisylvian) or whether it is located outside this network of language areas. The perisylvian area or zone contains Broca's area, Wernicke's area, the supramarginal and angular gyri, and the long association tracts that connect these language centers. The perisylvian aphasias are Broca's, Wernicke's, conduction, and global types. Extrasylvian or extra-perisylvian aphasias result from lesions to areas that lie outside of but project to the primary perisylvian language areas. From an anatomical perspective, extrasylvian aphasias are caused by lesions to border vascular areas between the anterior and middle cerebral arteries, and between the posterior and middle cerebral arteries. This border vascular area is also referred to as the *watershed zone*. Although perisylvian aphasias result in an impaired ability to repeat utterances, the extrasylvian aphasias are characterized by a preserved ability to repeat utterances (Table 1). Extrasylvian aphasias are the transcortical aphasias (motor, sensory, and mixed) as well as anomic aphasia (Beeson et al., 2004).

The "Boston" Classification and the Western Aphasia Battery Taxonomy

The BDAE (Goodglass et al., 2001) and WAB-R (Kertesz, 2007) taxonomies are similar and are based on profiling a client's performance on naming, auditory comprehension, fluency, and repetition. Based on these four key aspects of language function, eight types of aphasia syndromes can be identified (Table 1) and are discussed next.

Anomic Aphasia

Anomic aphasia is also referred to as amnestic aphasia. Davis (2000) describes this as the "mildest form of aphasia" (p. 38). Anomic aphasia may present as an isolated syndrome or may be a later stage of recovery from other aphasia syndromes such as Broca's, Wernicke's, conduction, or transcortical aphasia. Anomic aphasia is associated with minimal to mild impairment of auditory comprehension, fluent and grammatically correct utterances, and a pronounced impairment in the ability to retrieve words. This inability to retrieve words often results in frequent circumlocutions, semantic paraphasias (e.g., saying knife for butter), use of nonspecific or ambiguous nouns (e.g., "stuff," "thing," etc.), and use of pronouns without preceding nouns. For example, when asked in what city he lived, a client with anomic aphasia, RH, responded, "We live in ... live in ... what's-that-place ... wherever ... its not too far." When this same client was asked who referred him to our clinic, he responded, "You know whats-her-name referred us and thought it would be good for me to get more therapy."

Persons with anomic aphasia may present with variable performance on reading and writing tasks. In some instances, the word-finding difficulties also are revealed in client's writing performance. Anomia, by itself, is viewed as a poorly localizing symptom and the site of lesion causing it can vary considerably. However, this type of aphasia is most often associated with a lesion in the left angular gyrus, sparing Wernicke's area.

Table 1. Characteristics of the Major Aphasia Syndromes.

Type of Aphasia	Lesion Localization	Naming	Fluency	Repetition	Auditory Comprehension	Other Features
Anomic aphasia	Angular gyrus; possibly second temporal gyrus	Impaired	Fluent	Relatively preserved	Preserved	Frequent circumlocutions, few paraphasias
Broca's aphasia	Inferior frontal region, left insula, periventricular white matter	Impaired	Nonfluent	Impaired	Mild impairment (relatively preserved)	Agrammatic output, prosodic alterations
Conduction aphasia	Most commonly: supramarginal gyrus, arcuate fasiculus, posterior superior temporal gyrus, superior longitudinal fasiculus. Rarely: Wernicke's area, left insula, auditory association area	Impaired	Fluent	Impaired	Impaired	Frequent paraphasias
Wernicke's aphasia	Posterior third of the superior temporal gyrus (in the inferior distribution of the MCA), left insula	Impaired	Fluent	Impaired	Severely impaired	Frequent paraphasias, neologisms, jargon

Transcortical motor aphasia	Supplementary motor cortex, its underlying white matter pathways, left frontal lobe – anterior and superior to Broca's area	Impaired	Nonfluent	Preserved	Mild impairment (relatively spared)	Naming ability much better than spontaneous speech
Transcortical sensory aphasia	Parietotemporal lesions (not involving Wernicke's area)	Impaired	Fluent	Preserved	Severely impaired	Frequent paraphasias, similar to those in Wernicke's aphasia
Transcortical mixed aphasia or Isolation aphasia	Anterior and posterior association areas in the left hemisphere	Impaired	Nonfluent, except when repeating utterances	Preserved relative to spontaneous speech	Moderately to severely impaired	Echolalia may be present
Global aphasia	Large perisylvian lesions that encompass Broca's and Wernicke's areas, extending deep into white matter	Severely impaired	Severely impaired	Severely impaired	Severely impaired	Stereotypical utterances (sometimes with normal intonation and melody)

Broca's Aphasia

Broca's area is an area in the posterior inferior frontal lobe, named after Paul Broca, the French neurologist who first identified the behavioral symptoms associated with damage to this region (Brookshire, 2007). Broca's aphasia results from a lesion to this region and/or surrounding cortex. Broca's aphasia is sometimes described as expressive aphasia or motor aphasia. Typical symptoms of Broca's aphasia include moderately to severely nonfluent speech, mild to moderate impairments of auditory comprehension, and better preserved naming ability as compared to sentence formulation ability. Apraxia of speech (AOS) is also quite common in persons with Broca's aphasia.

The nonfluent speech in Broca's aphasia is characterized by agrammatism or telegraphic speech. Agrammatism is a pattern of speech production in which grammar is relatively inaccessible and individuals make grammatical errors, struggle to form sentences, omit grammatical morphemes yet may be able to convey meaning using strings of nouns (O'Connor, Anema, Datta, Signorelli, & Obler, 2005). It is common for functor words and inflectional affixes to be omitted or substituted.

For example, when a client, JM, who has agrammatism, was asked about what happened when he had his stroke, he replied "Head ... ow ... ow .... nothing there (as he pointed to his mouth)... down ... floor ... ow ... ow ... pain ... friend ... hospital."

This brief sample illustrates that individuals with agrammatism have difficulty producing articles, prepositions, pronouns, and auxiliary verbs. According to Thompson (2001), in addition to these marked impairments in sentence production, persons with agrammatism also have difficulty comprehending syntactically complex sentences such as passive sentences (e.g., "The girl was teased by her brother") and object relative clauses (e.g., "The grandmother saw the brother who teased his sister"). Further, agrammatic individuals with aphasia also struggle to comprehend semantically reversible sentences and sentences with complex or multiple verbs.

Historically, Broca's aphasia has been associated with damage to the inferior frontal gyrus, specifically to the opercular and triangular parts of this gyrus. Anatomically, this area is referred to as Broca's area (Brodmann's area 44). Recently, researchers have demonstrated that the symptoms associated with Broca's aphasia may occur because of damage anywhere from directly involving Broca's area to its underlying white matter, premotor and motor areas adjacent to Broca's area, to the anterior part of the insula, or to the basal ganglia (Damasio, 1991; Dronkers, 1996).

Wernicke's Aphasia

Wernicke's aphasia was first described by Carl Wernicke in 1874 and often is regarded as the most severe type of fluent aphasia (Davis, 2000). Wernicke's aphasia is characterized by moderate to severe auditory comprehension impairments and the spared ability to speak fluently and effortlessly in syntactically correct sentences. However, the spontaneous speech of persons with Wernicke's aphasia contains excessive jargon, neologisms (nonwords that may or may not be phonologically related or similar to the intended target word), and numerous paraphasias that completely obscure any meaningful content. For this reason, sometimes the term *jargon aphasia* is used to refer to Wernicke's aphasia. Individuals with Wernicke's aphasia are often unaware of their errors and unable to benefit from any auditory-verbal feedback about their errors.

Wernicke's aphasia is associated with lesions involving the posterior two-thirds of the left superior temporal gyrus (Brodmann's area 22) and also lesions extending involving the inferior parietal lobule (Brodmann's areas 39 and 40). Damasio (2001) suggests that Wernicke's aphasia also may result from lesions extending into the posterior parts of the middle and inferior temporal gyri (Brodmann's areas 37, 20, and 21).

Conduction Aphasia

Conduction aphasia is a relatively rare aphasia syndrome and is thought to account for less than 10% of individuals who have been diagnosed with aphasia (Bhatnagar & Andy, 1995). Geschwind (1965) described conduction aphasia as a *disconnection syndrome* in which impairments resulted from the disrupted connections between anatomical centers that are intact and have no structural lesions. In conduction aphasia, the most likely neuroanatomical location of this disrupted connection is the supramarginal gyrus (Brodmann's area 40) and its underlying white matter, which includes the arcuate fasciculus, a band of association fibers that functionally connect Broca's area (Brodmann's area 44) and Wernicke's area (Brodmann's area 22). Conduction aphasia also has been reported to occur from lesions to the left auditory cortex and the insula (Damasio & Damasio, 1980), without damage to the supramarginal gyrus, as well as from lesions involving the posterior part of the superior temporal gyrus or Wernicke's area proper (Alexander, 1999).

The hallmark of conduction aphasia is an individual's severe inability to repeat utterances and impaired phonemic production and phonological output assembly (Alexander, 1999). This is in contrast with better spontaneous speech and auditory comprehension abilities. Word retrieval deficits are also prominent, and spontaneous verbal output is fluent but contains many paraphasias.

Global Aphasia
Global aphasia is also referred to as *total aphasia* (Love & Webb, 1996, p. 208) and is characterized by severely impaired expressive and receptive language abilities including reading and writing. Helm-Estabrooks and Albert (2004a, p. 253) describe global aphasia as the most devastating type of aphasia. Individuals with global aphasia often present with verbal stereotypies and use facial expressions, nonlinguistic vocal behaviors, or manual gestures to communicate. Several individuals with global aphasia also present with oromotor and limb apraxia which limits nonverbal expression even through gesturing and drawing. Global aphasia often is associated with large lesions encompassing the entire perisylvian region. Such lesions often result from occlusion of the middle cerebral artery, before it divides further. This has the effect of causing extensive damage to frontal, parietal, and temporal regions of the brain.

Transcortical Motor Aphasia
Transcortical motor aphasia (TCMA) is most similar to Broca's aphasia with the exception of relatively spared repetition ability. So an individual with TCMA would present with nonfluent spontaneous speech and mildly impaired auditory comprehension, but would be able to repeat utterances accurately without difficulty. According to Berthier (1999), TCMA results from frontal lobe lesions located superior and anterior to Broca's area. Further, the size of the lesion tends to be smaller than that seen in classic Broca's aphasia. Per Goodglass et al. (2001), the fluent/nonfluent distinction is not particularly applicable to this aphasia type because a client with TCMA is capable of producing an accurately articulated and grammatically correct utterance.

Transcortical Sensory Aphasia
Transcortical sensory aphasia (TCSA) is a rare type of fluent aphasia, the main characteristic of which is well-preserved repetition ability in the absence of functional auditory comprehension or propositional speech. Reading, writing, and naming abilities also are poor. The site of lesion in TCSA is thought to be deep and posterior to Wernicke's area either involving the angular gyrus (Brodmann's area 39) or the posterior part of the middle temporal gyrus (Brodmann's area 37). Helm-Estabrooks and Albert (2004a) suggest that the syndrome of transcortical sensory aphasia is

very similar to the language deficits seen in individuals with Alzheimer's disease (AD). However, it is important to note that linguistic deficits in persons with AD vary considerably from the very early stages to the early and middle stages of the disease. Although an individual with moderate stage AD may show significant overlap of symptoms with a client who has TCSA, an individual with early stage AD may not present with symptoms similar to TCSA in type or severity and may have a profile more like anomic aphasia.

Transcortical Mixed Aphasia
Transcortical mixed aphasia (TMA) is sometimes referred to as the *isolation syndrome* (Bhatnagar & Andy, 1995) and involves a combination of the lesions involved in TCSA and TCMA, described earlier. The term isolation syndrome reflects that an intact perisylvian language system has become disconnected from other cortical areas necessary for language comprehension or meaningful propositional speech. A client presenting with symptoms of TMA cannot comprehend spoken language, speak fluently, name objects, read, or write. However, clients with TMA are able to repeat utterances fluently and also frequently exhibit echolalia.

RARE APHASIAS

Subcortical Aphasia

These aphasia syndromes are associated with subcortical or principally subcortical sites of lesion including the thalamus, the putamen, the head of the caudate nucleus, and parts of the internal capsule (Table 2). Three

Table 2. Lesion Localization in Rare Aphasia Syndromes.

Type of Rare Aphasia	Lesion Localization
Subcortical aphasia	Thalamus, head of the caudate nucleus, anterior capsule, posterior capsule, and putamen
Crossed aphasia	Nondominant cerebral hemisphere
Primary progressive aphasia (PPA)	Left perisylvian area, specifically frontal, temporal, and parietal regions
Prefrontal aphasia	Left dorsolateral prefrontal cortex, encompassing Brodmann's areas 9, 10, and 46

subcortical aphasia types have been reported in the literature, including thalamic aphasia, anterior capsular or putaminal aphasia, and posterior capsular or putaminal aphasia (Alexander, Naeser, & Palumbo, 1987; Helm-Estabrooks & Albert, 2004a). All three subcortical aphasia types are characterized by anomia, paraphasias variable mean phrase length (between six to eight words), and hypophonia or reduced vocal volume. Although thalamic and anterior capsular aphasias are associated with relatively good repetition ability, posterior capsular aphasias are not. Auditory comprehension is variable in thalamic aphasias, is relatively spared in anterior capsular aphasias, and is poor in posterior capsular aphasias.

Crossed Aphasia

Crossed aphasia is a rare type of aphasia in which language impairments occur following a right (nondominant) hemisphere lesion in an individual who is right handed. In other words, crossed aphasia occurs after a lesion that is ipsilateral to the patient's dominant hand. In general, the language impairments resulting from crossed aphasia are similar to those seen in the classic aphasia syndromes resulting from left-hemisphere CVAs. However, Paghera, Marien, and Vignolo (2003) suggest that in some individuals with crossed aphasia, the language problems typically associated with damage to the left hemisphere may co-occur with the cognitive-communicative impairments usually observed in individuals with right-hemisphere CVAs (e.g., neglect syndrome, anosognosia, etc.). Recently, Coppens, Hungerford, Yamaguchi, and Yamadori (2002) have reported that crossed aphasia may result from multiple lesions in the right hemisphere. (For a recent review on the syndrome of crossed aphasia, the reader is referred to Sheehy (2006).)

Primary Progressive Aphasia (PPA)

This syndrome of "slowly progressive aphasia" was first described by Marsel Mesulam in 1982. McNeil and Duffy (2001) define PPA as an insidious, gradually progressive aphasia with a prolonged course, resulting from a neurodegenerative process that typically involves the left perisylvian region of the brain (Table 2). Individuals with PPA are often misdiagnosed as having AD or manic-depressive psychosis. PPA is now regarded as a distinct clinical variant of frontotemporal lobar degeneration or frontotemporal dementia. Recently, Mesulam (2006) described PPA as a focal neurodegenerative syndrome characterized by an isolated and gradual dissolution of word finding and word usage. In order to make a diagnosis of PPA, a client must present with isolated language impairment, in the absence of cognitive deficits, for at least two years. Further, Mesulam emphasizes that a client with PPA should not demonstrate any signs or symptoms of a focal lesion. Further, an individual with PPA must not present with personality changes, or have concomitant impairments of memory or visuospatial function. Language disturbances must be the most salient deficit in PPA and often present as the main obstacle in carrying out activities of daily living (ADLs).

Dynamic or Prefrontal Aphasia

Several researchers have recently documented the effect of damage to the prefrontal cortex (PFC) on language and cognitive function (Alexander, 2002; Gabrieli, Poldrack, & Desmond, 1998; Mesulam, 2000). The term *dynamic aphasia* (also prefrontal aphasia) has been used to describe the language impairments resulting from lesions to the prefrontal cortex. According to Frattali and Grafman (2005), dynamic aphasia is caused by lesions to the dorsolateral prefrontal cortex, specifically involving Brodmann's areas 9, 10, and 46 (Table 2).

Dynamic aphasia can result from right- or left-hemisphere lesions; however, observed deficits are greater in left-hemisphere and bilateral lesions. This type of aphasia is characterized by a triad of hallmark features which include: (1) a significant reduction in the amount of spontaneous speech and its length and complexity, (2) a lack of initiation and a restricted range of narrative expression, and (3) a loss of verbal fluency. These three distinctive features are observed in the absence of articulatory or speech motor programming impairments, auditory comprehension deficits, syntactic impairments, and semantic and phonemic paraphasias typically associated with aphasia. Further, patients with damage to the PFC and resulting language impairments present with a lack of spontaneity and creativity in their verbal responses, difficulty performing on tasks requiring sustained verbal effort, selective attention deficits, lack of drive, and apathy. Ferstl, Guthke, and von Cramon (1999) suggest that damage to the PFC causes language impairments resulting from primary cognitive impairments in action planning, attention, working memory, preparatory set, and inhibitory set.

APHASIA SYNDROMES: TO CLASSIFY OR
NOT TO CLASSIFY

Most aphasia batteries typically used by clinicians and researchers (e.g., the WAB-R, the BDAE, or the Porch Index of Communicative Abilities (PICA)) are instrumental in identifying the presence of and determining the severity of aphasia, as well as classifying a client's profile of spared and impaired language abilities as a distinct aphasia type. Such classification systems are based on identifying clinically meaningful associations between specific signs and/or symptoms involving language function and a likely neuroanatomical lesion responsible for producing them. Damasio (1998) describes the classification of aphasia syndromes as a necessary evil because of several limitations inherent in commonly used classification systems. These limitations are discussed next.

First, not all clients with aphasia present with patterns of language impairment that fit neatly with a particular type of aphasia (Murray & Clark, 2006). For instance, because most aphasia syndromes are defined based on the presence of multiple criteria for present impairments or spared abilities, it becomes difficult to classify syndromes when not all the criteria are fulfilled. Helm-Estabrooks and Albert (2004a) estimate that 10–15% of clients with aphasia present with patterns of impairment that do not fit the description of the typical aphasia syndromes. Some possible reasons for a client presenting with an unusual or atypical symptom profile may be lesions in both hemispheres, prior history of a head injury, seizure disorder, substance abuse, or other psychiatric disorder, or left-handedness or ambidexterity suggesting atypical cerebral dominance.

Second, some dichotomous classifications (e.g., receptive versus expressive) are confusing at best and erroneous at worst, given that clients with aphasia typically present with *both* receptive and expressive language impairments, albeit in varying degrees of severity. Further, classifying a client as having a distinct type of aphasia is not helpful for understanding the specific nature of breakdown in the client's linguistic systems (e.g., in semantics versus the phonological output lexicon). Then there is the issue of two clients who happen to obtain similar scores on a particular subtest but could well have completely different underlying mechanisms resulting in their specific impairments.

Another issue with aphasia classification systems is that the strict localizationist perspective relating specific aphasia types to distinct neuronatomical lesions has been called into question repeatedly. For example, Dronkers, Shapiro, Redfern, and Knight (1992) reported that it was possible to have damage to Broca's area without resulting symptoms of Broca's aphasia, and that damage to areas besides Broca's area (e.g., to the insula) could result in symptoms of classic Broca's aphasia (Dronkers, 1993). Another source of evidence against strict localization theories is that clients with aphasia often evolve from one aphasic syndrome to another over time (e.g., a client with Broca's aphasia may evolve to a profile of anomic aphasia) despite the underlying neuroanatomical lesion remaining unchanged. Finally, from the perspective of planning treatment, merely identifying the type of aphasia does not help in identifying relevant therapy goals or determining which intervention techniques are most appropriate for a particular client.

COMMUNICATION INTERVENTION APPROACHES IN APHASIA

The World Health Organization's International Classification of Functioning, Disability, and Health (ICF) (World Health Organization, 2001) is a comprehensive framework for describing the states of human functioning and disability (Fig. 1). According to this framework, two major components

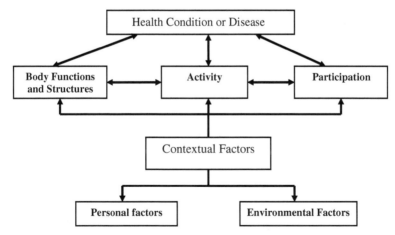

Fig. 1. International Classification of Functioning, Disability, and Health (adapted from WHO, 2001).

must be considered in evaluating the impact of a health condition or disease on an individual, and planning for appropriate intervention. The first component is *Functioning and Disability*, which has two parts: (a) body functions and structures and (b) activity and participation. *Body functions and structures* refer to physiological and psychological functions of body systems. The term *activity* refers to the ability of an individual to perform a specific task or action, and the term *participation* refers to an individual's involvement in a life situation. The second component of the ICF model is *contextual factors*, which consist of personal and environmental factors. Environmental factors refer to the physical, social, and attitudinal environments in which a person resides and can positively or adversely affect an individual's functioning. Personal factors are those factors that are not directly related to the health condition or disease experienced by the individual, for example, age, gender, ethnicity, educational status, and lifestyle of a person.

This ICF framework is helpful in conceptualizing the myriad intervention approaches used for persons with aphasia. Some intervention approaches may target enhancing physiological and psychological functioning of body systems. For example, the use of pharmacological agents such as tissue plasminogen activators (TPA) to dissolve stroke-causing blood clots is an example of an intervention that influences body structures and functioning. Another example is treatments that target oromotor movements, which may reduce the severity of a client's dysarthria or improve the degree of speech intelligibility of a person with aphasia. Other intervention approaches may target enhancing the performance of an individual with aphasia on specific tasks (activity) or in specific situations and roles (participation). For example, a model-based approach to train grapheme to phoneme production may enhance the ability of an individual with aphasia to write words, thus impacting their ability to perform an activity. If this individual then receives another situation-specific intervention because of which they can now write a shopping list for their caregiver or write a short note in a greeting card, then being able to write words now facilitates his/her independence in communication, quality of life, and allows for participation in a variety of life roles.

There are multiple dichotomies to characterize the wide variety of intervention approaches in aphasia. In this section, a brief overview of some widely used dichotomies is provided, followed by a discussion of specific intervention approaches for persons with aphasia.

GENERAL CONCEPTUAL APPROACHES TO APHASIA INTERVENTION

The following general dichotomies can be used to classify intervention approaches for any communicative disorder, including aphasia. These dichotomies are

1. direct versus indirect interventions,
2. individual versus group interventions,
3. restorative versus compensatory interventions, and
4. process-based versus situation-specific therapeutic interventions.

Direct versus Indirect Interventions

Direct interventions are those in which a speech-language pathologist intervenes with persons with aphasia individually or in groups (Mahendra, 2001) to enhance their communicative functioning, independence, and quality of life. Indirect interventions (Hopper, 2001) are designed to improve the communicative and cognitive function of individuals with aphasia by addressing caregiver education and training (e.g., in-services for professionals and family training), establishing environmental supports and modifications, and developing therapeutic routines.

Individual versus Group Interventions

Treatment approaches differ in whether the person with aphasia is participating in a one-on-one intervention or a group intervention. Individual speech and language therapy typically focuses on didactic therapy tasks designed for maximizing linguistic and cognitive recovery. In individual speech therapy, treatment tasks typically target impaired modalities and gains on these tasks often are reported as a result of therapy. However, generalization to real-life, functional, communication situations may be difficult to achieve. Group treatment for persons with aphasia has become popular given the growing evidence base for its efficacy and effectiveness (Aten, Caligiuri, & Holland, 1982; Avent, 1997; Bollinger, Musson, & Holland, 1993; Holland & Beeson, 1999). Further, group therapy is a viable method of service delivery in the current managed-care environment in which receiving reimbursement for speech therapy services has become increasingly challenging. Elman (2006) cites several advantages of group treatment over individual treatment with regard to:

- promoting better generalization of trained strategies to real-life settings,
- providing a socially stimulating and supportive situation that provides opportunities for diverse communicative interactions with peers and group facilitators,
- improving the psychosocial functioning of clients with aphasia, and
- being more cost-effective as compared to individual therapy.

Restorative versus Compensatory Interventions

Many authorities (Albert, Goodglass, Helm, Rubens, & Alexander, 1981; Whitworth, Webster, & Howard, 2005) classify aphasia intervention approaches into two main types – restorative (restitutive) and compensatory (substitutive). This dichotomy is based on differing beliefs about the nature of impairment resulting from aphasia and on the intended target of therapy techniques. Restorative approaches are based on the view that aphasia is an impairment of the access to linguistic knowledge because of damage to language representations. The goal of restorative interventions then is to restore or retrain a person with aphasia to access language representations. Compensatory approaches, however, are based on the view that aphasia is not just a problem of access to language representations but that the language processes in persons with aphasia are irreparably damaged and cannot be restored. Therefore, therapy focuses on compensatory strategies (e.g., using other communication modalities such as gestures, or drawing) to bypass impaired language functions.

Process-Based versus Situation-Specific Therapeutic Interventions

Process-based therapy approaches are aimed at training strategies and responses for application to a wide variety of situations or behaviors. Some examples of process-based approaches are using a cueing hierarchy to facilitate single-word writing performance in persons with aphasia or using a combination of semantic and phonological cueing to enhance word retrieval of names of trained exemplars of a category. In contrast, situation-specific therapy approaches (Hopper & Holland, 1998) focus on a communicative need in a specific context, for example writing a note in a greeting card, being able to comprehend and provide input during a conversation with a spouse, or being able to verbally communicate the nature of an emergency to a 911 operator. The goal of situation-specific therapy is to train a fixed set of specific responses to a predictable sequence of events in a functional situation. An excellent example of this is provided in a study conducted by Hopper and Holland (1998) in which they used a single subject experimental design to train two adults with Broca's aphasia to communicate verbally in simulated emergency situations.

SPECIFIC APPROACHES TO APHASIA INTERVENTION

Having discussed the aforementioned general approaches to aphasia intervention, specific approaches to aphasia therapy are presented in this section (Table 3). These fall into two categories – *traditional* approaches and

Table 3. Classification of Aphasia Therapy Approaches.

General approaches
1. Direct versus indirect interventions
2. Individual versus group interventions
3. Restorative versus compensatory interventions
4. Process-based versus situation specific interventions
Specific approaches
1. Traditional approaches
  a. Stimulation approaches
    i. Melodic intonation therapy
    ii. Visual action therapy
  b. Cognitive neuropsychological and neurolinguistic approaches
    i. Semantic feature analysis
    ii. Mapping therapy
  c. Technology-based therapy approaches
    i. Augmentative and alternative communication systems
    ii. Aphasia therapy software
2. Social and life participation approaches to intervention
  a. PACE therapy
  b. Conversational coaching and scripting
  c. Reciprocal scaffolding treatment

psychosocial or functional approaches (Chapey, 2001). For both traditional and psychosocial approaches, subcategories of these approaches are presented first, followed by detailed discussion of a few selected examples of each subcategory.

Traditional Approaches

Stimulation Approaches

Stimulation approaches were pioneered by Hildred Schuell in the 1960s. Schuell proposed that a short period of intensive auditory stimulation would result in an improvement in the language abilities of a person with aphasia. She focused exclusively on the auditory modality reasoning that language was most dependent on it. Since Schuell's early work, it is now known that persons with aphasia benefit from input in other sensory modalities (visual, tactile, etc.) and not just input restricted to the auditory modality. This has led to a multimodality approach to rehabilitation of language and communicative function in aphasia (Duffy & Coelho, 2001). LaPointe (1985) introduced the notion of programmed stimulation, refining and extending the concept of stimulation as an approach to therapy for persons with aphasia. The term "programmed stimulation" reflects emphasis on a systematic or hierarchical approach to cognitive stimulation for persons with aphasia. According to Davis (2007), programmed stimulation approaches have the following characteristics:

• Specific goals are selected for intervention, with identified initial behaviors and terminal response criteria.
• Goals are broken down into a sequence of task components, arranged from least to greatest difficulty or complexity.
• Intervention is structured to proceed from maximal dependence on the clinician to maximal independence of the client.

   Some classic examples of programmed stimulation therapy approaches for aphasia are melodic intonation therapy (MIT) (Albert, Sparks, & Helm, 1973; Helm-Estabrooks & Albert, 2004b; Sparks, 2001) and visual action therapy (VAT) (Helm-Estabrooks, Fitzpatrick & Barresi, 1982). These two approaches are discussed next.

Melodic Intonation Therapy.   MIT (Albert et al., 1973; Helm-Estabrooks & Albert, 2004b; Sparks, 2001) is a structured therapy program intended to facilitate verbal expression in clients with aphasia who have severely impaired verbal output despite relatively spared auditory comprehension. This therapy is based on the systematic observation that some individuals with severe nonfluent aphasias are able to produce words accurately in the context of singing as opposed to propositional speech. Another rationale for the use of melodic intonation to facilitate verbal expression in nonfluent individuals with aphasia is that these individuals have an intact right hemisphere, which is specialized for processing music and prosody. It is important to note that melodic intonation is not the same as singing. Rather, melodic intonation is based on the typical prosody of spoken utterances. Typical prosody used during spontaneous speech has three elements – pitch variation (or melodic line) within a phrase or sentence, tempo and rhythm changes during an utterance, and stress placement on different words of an utterance to signal emphasis.

MIT is hierarchically organized into three levels of increasing complexity. The first two levels target a client's ability to produce single multisyllabic words and short, predictable phrases, respectively. At the third level, sentences of greater length and increased phonological complexity are introduced. For a detailed description of the rationale and methodology of MIT, determining candidacy, steps involved at each level, and detailed scoring procedures, the reader is directed to Helm-Estabrooks and Albert (2004b) and Sparks (2001).

Visual Action Therapy.   VAT (Helm-Estabrooks et al., 1982) is a therapy program designed to improve the nonverbal communication of individuals with severe expressive aphasia. The purpose of VAT then is to teach individuals to use gestures instead of words for independent, functional communication. VAT is a three-phase program; each phase has three levels of training. At each of the three levels, there is a hierarchically ordered sequence of steps that facilitate a client's spontaneous use of visual gestures for communication. The three phases of VAT target production of proximal gestures (e.g., using a whole-arm movement to strike a hammer), distal gestures (e.g., using hand and finger movements to write with a pencil), and oral gestures (e.g., to suck liquid through a straw), respectively. At each phase, a client begins at Level 1 with using real objects, pictures of these objects, and pictures of the actions used with these objects. In a series of nine steps, Level 1 activities lead the client from matching pictures and real objects (Step 1) to producing gestures for hidden objects (Step 9). At Level 2, the client uses only the action pictures without real objects and begins from observing demonstrations of pantomimed gestures (Step 5) through recognizing (Step 6) and producing them (Step 7) to independent production of gestures for hidden action pictures (Step 9). Similarly, at Level 3, the client proceeds through the same sequence of steps described in Level 2 but using only the pictures of the objects (not their actions) as cues.

Cognitive Neuropsychological and Neurolinguistic Approaches
The aim of cognitive neuropsychological research is to develop models of typical language processes, involved in specific language tasks such as lexical semantic processing or sentence formulation. Cognitive neuropsychological and neurolinguistic approaches for aphasia intervention utilize information processing models that offer clinicians and researchers a theoretical foundation for understanding normal cognitive-linguistic processing and for identifying impaired cognitive-linguistic processes in persons with aphasia. These models provide a sound basis for identifying the mechanisms and component representations necessary to perform a particular language task (see Fig. 2 for an example of an information processing model for lexical processing). Based on this understanding and analyzing a client's performance on a task, the client's underlying impaired and spared cognitive processes at each stage of a model can be identified. According to Hillis (2001), this knowledge then helps a clinician to design interventions that either target improving or restoring impaired cognitive processes (restitutive treatments) or by compensating for the impaired processes by relying more on spared abilities (substitutive treatments). Such model-based treatment approaches primarily focus on intervening at an impairment level (per the ICF model) for a client's deficits.

Semantic Feature Analysis.   One example of a treatment to facilitate word retrieval in persons with aphasia is semantic feature analysis (SFA) (Boyle & Coelho, 1995). SFA (Boyle, 2001; Boyle & Coelho, 1995; Coelho, McHugh, & Boyle, 2000; Lowell, Beeson, & Holland, 1995; Rider, Wright, Marshall, & Page, 2008) is a cueing technique based on an understanding of the cognitive architecture of semantic representations. During SFA therapy, the client is encouraged to produce exemplars that are semantically related to a target word, in order to facilitate its retrieval. The use of semantic cues in SFA therapy is based on the view of semantic memory as a hierarchically organized system. In this semantic system, conceptual knowledge is stored in the form of an associative network in which related concepts, events, and words are linked. Repeated activation of a target word, for example "Halloween," activates related nodes or concepts such as "pumpkins," "costumes," "trick or treating," etc. Similarly,

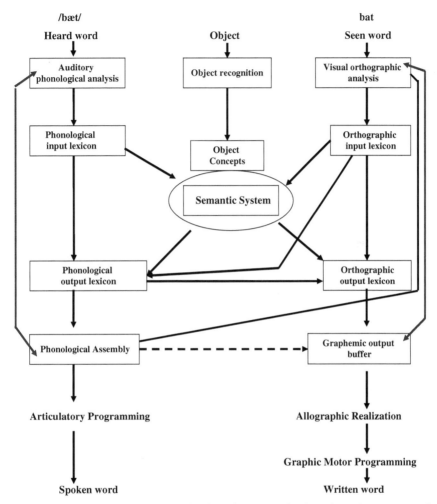

Fig. 2. Language-Processing Model for Single Words (based on Patterson and Shewell's (1987) logogen model).

repeatedly accessing or producing semantically related words to a target word facilitates retrieval of the intended word. During SFA therapy, a client is shown a picture (e.g., a rose) and asked to name it. Following stimulus presentation, regardless of a correct or incorrect response, a scheme is used (Fig. 3) to help the client to generate semantic features about a rose such as

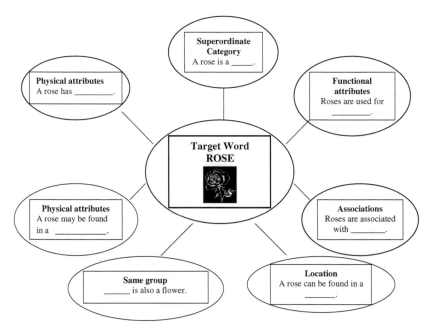

Fig. 3.   Example of a Matrix Used for Semantic Feature Analysis Therapy.

its superordinate category (flower), physical attributes (fragrance, color, and thorns), functional attributes (in bouquets, for decoration, worn in the hair, etc.), and associations (Valentine's day, a date, etc.). If the client is unable to produce these details, the clinician provides them. Then the client is asked to rename the target picture. The SFA technique facilitates semantic activation of related information, which in turn makes the target word more accessible for retrieval. Another benefit of using SFA is that clients can learn how to describe attributes or features of a target object as a self-cueing strategy in a communicative interaction.

Mapping Therapy for Agrammatic Aphasia.   Mapping therapy (Schwartz, Saffran, Fink, Myers, & Martin, 1994) is grounded in linguistic theory, and targets sentence comprehension and production impairments observed in individuals with agrammatic aphasia. Mapping therapy is based on a theoretical explanation for agrammatism as "a deficit in mapping semantics onto syntax" (Thompson, 2001, p. 609) and remediation of this mapping deficit by focusing on comprehension and production of sentence noun phrases and their thematic roles in simple (S-V-O) and complex (passive and object relative) sentences. The treatment of underlying forms approach (see Shapiro, 1997 for an excellent review) is similar to mapping therapy in its focus on thematic role assignment and its use in simple and complex sentences. However, this approach also builds on mapping therapy by adding operations that focus on establishing trace-antecedent relations in complex sentences.

Another difference between mapping therapy and the treatment of underlying forms approach is that the latter focuses on training more complex structures before simpler ones and emphasizes generalization to untreated sentences (of the same type as treated sentences but with different forms).

Technology-Based Approaches
The pervasive use of and recent advancements in computer technology have led to reduced costs of hardware and software components as well as the widespread availability of innovative, user-friendly, computer applications that can be used by persons with aphasia. Computers and AAC systems are viable media for enabling clients to develop functional communication skills, especially when regaining verbal expression abilities may not be realistic. Two examples of technology-based approaches are presented below. Augmentative and alternative communication (AAC) systems are discussed first followed by a discussion of aphasia treatment software.

Augmentative and Alternative Communication (AAC). Many persons with mild to moderate language impairments resulting from aphasia respond well to a variety of approaches for speech and language therapy. However, some individuals with greater severity of language impairments are not able to communicate independently and effectively using the verbal modality, even after intensive speech and language therapy. For such individuals, AAC techniques and strategies are an ideal compensatory approach to intervention. Such techniques may or may not involve use of technology. Training persons with aphasia to independently communicate using an AAC technique is a perfect example of a life participation approach that emphasizes effective functional communication. The American Speech Language Hearing Association (ASHA, 2005) defines AAC as "An area of research, clinical, and educational practice that involves investigation of and compensating for *temporary or permanent impairments, activity limitations,* and *participation restrictions* in individuals with severe disorders of speech-language production and/or comprehension, including spoken and written modes of communication." The goal of using AAC systems with clients who have aphasia is to help them develop multiple modalities for independent and effective communication and to train partners to validate such multimodality communication (Buzolich, 2006, pp. 4–12), while providing functional communication therapy in a natural context. The strong point of using AAC systems as a therapeutic approach is the ability to address body functions, activities, and participation simultaneously.

There are multiple AAC options to choose from depending on the profile of spared and impaired abilities of a client with aphasia, the severity of their communication impairment, and considerations about associated financial costs (Lytton, 2005; Elman, 2005). These include:

- Unaided options: Examples include using manual signs, gestures, or finger spelling.
- Technology-based AAC options: These options include use of speech generating devices (SGDs) and software programs that turn computers into speech output communication devices. SGDs are generally used as a part of a comprehensive AAC treatment package (Koul, Petroi, & Schlosser, 2010; Koul & Corwin, 2003).
- No-technology-based AAC options: These options do not involve the production of synthetic or digitized speech output upon selection of a message. Communication books and boards, written-choice communication, alphabet cards, and photographs are examples of no-technology AAC options (Beukelman & Mirenda, 2005; Ho, Weiss, Garrett, & Lloyd, 2005; Koul & Corwin, 2003).

Aphasia Treatment Software. Aphasia treatment software refers to commercially available software applications or packages that allow clinicians to select and use diverse stimuli for simple and complex language tasks. Some examples of useful software applications are Parrot Software (1981–2007), Bungalow software (1995–2006), Adult Aphasia and Traumatic Brain Injury Package (from Laureate Learning Systems®), and the TheraSimplicity™ (©1997–2007) Software Library. Such packages are easy to use, incorporate a unique selection of stimuli/tasks, and allow clinicians to easily implement individualized interventions. Further, such packages also can be made available to clients for structured practice in their home environments.

Psychosocial and Functional Approaches to Aphasia Intervention

Social and Life Participation Approaches to Aphasia Therapy
Social and life participation approaches to aphasia intervention address the activity and participation levels of the WHO model. Such approaches address the everyday communicative needs of persons with aphasia and play a critical role in enhancing their quality of life by positively influencing their information exchanges (or transactions) with communication partners, social interactions, and societal participation. In order for social approaches for aphasia therapy to be successful, treatment must:

- be conducted in a naturalistic and personally meaningful context,
- emphasize the reciprocal and transactional nature of communication,
- focus on the social characteristics of communication, and
- increase the individual's participation in different contexts in their everyday life (Avent, 1997; Lyon & Shadden, 2001; Simmons-Mackie, 2001).

Three representative examples of social and life participation approaches to aphasia intervention are discussed below:

Promoting Aphasic's Communicative Effectiveness. Promoting Aphasic's Communicative Effectiveness (PACE) (Davis & Wilcox, 1981, 1985; Davis, 2005) is a widely used therapy program for aphasia, which emphasizes naturalistic social interaction for enhancing the communicative abilities of individuals with aphasia. According to Davis (2005), PACE was developed based on two cardinal assumptions. The first assumption is that persons with aphasia, despite their communicative impairment, still possess residual communicative abilities. The second assumption is that opportunities for natural conversation allow individuals with aphasia the ability to be challenged by and to overcome communicative difficulties. The basic foundation of PACE therapy is reciprocity (i.e., the clinician and the individual with aphasia are equal participants in conversation and are each responsible for sharing the sender and receiver roles in a communicative interaction). PACE is based on four basic principles (Davis, 2000, 2005):

- Principle 1: Equal participation: In effective communicative interactions, a speaker and listener typically take turns conveying ideas and neither one dominates the interaction. During PACE therapy, this principle is employed to encourage an individual with aphasia to "share the floor" as a communicator, with the clinician. Both clinician and client take turns as senders and receivers of messages and are equally responsible for the success of their communicative interaction. This implies that each person must be an active participant in all roles of being a communicator (i.e., speaking, listening, asking questions for clarification, and providing feedback to each other).

- Principle 2: Exchanging new information: Based on PACE therapy guidelines, a clinician and client must exchange new information that is not previously known to the client or the clinician. This renders the communicative exchange more natural and ecologically valid in that the clinician does not already know what the client is describing or naming. Typically, PACE therapy involves a hierarchy of describing objects, then verbs, and finally parts of a story depicted on cards. The client and clinician take turns drawing a card and explaining its contents to each other.

- Principle 3: Freedom of choice of communicative modality: This principle stipulates that the focus of PACE therapy should be on communicative success rather than directing the use of a specific modality to communicate. Murray and Clark (2006, p. 355) consider this the most important principle of PACE therapy. Participants in PACE conversations may convey their idea by speaking, signing, writing a word, drawing, pointing, or pantomiming. This principle is critical so that an individual with aphasia uses any modality available to him or her in order to communicate successfully. If a client is unsuccessfully trying to communicate verbally and does not attempt to use another modality, the clinician can model different modalities for the client to help expand their repertoire of communicative strategies.

- Principle 4: Natural feedback: The final principle of PACE therapy is that the receiver provides feedback in an ongoing and natural way to indicate whether the sender's message was understood. Instead of telling the client that their response was correct or incorrect, the focus is on whether the message was understood or not. For instance, if a client produces a vague response, the clinician should indicate that they did not understand, followed by asking for clarification, requesting more information, guess at the intended message, or suggest that the client use an alternative strategy.

Conversational Coaching and Scripting. These approaches utilize scripted conversations, verbal and nonverbal strategies, systematic practice, and continuous clinician feedback to improve communicative interactions between clients with aphasia and their spouses, family members, caregivers, or volunteer communication partners. For example, a client with aphasia may work on a monologue script for introducing themselves to a stranger at a social event or making a toast at a family wedding or on a dialogue script to be able to have a productive phone conversation or to order their breakfast at a restaurant. To implement these interventions, the client and clinician work collaboratively to identify a situation for which a script must be generated. Depending on the client's profile of spared and impaired language modalities, the script may be written out or designed using keywords with pictures, drawings, or photographs (Elman, 2005). Additionally, a spouse, family member, or caregiver may also participate in being trained by the clinician to provide appropriate feedback to the person with aphasia and to use supportive strategies such as written cues, allowing increased talking time, or asking a simple yes–no clarification question. In one example of the use of conversational coaching, Hopper, Holland, and Rewega (2002) used this approach to enhance the communicative interactions between two individuals with aphasia and their spouses by providing training on facilitative behaviors. In another instance, Lyon and colleagues (1997) paired individuals with aphasia and volunteers from the community and taught the latter verbal and nonverbal strategies to facilitate communication. Similarly, Youmans, Holland, Munoz, and Bourgeois (2010) documented the benefits of using scripts to enhance automatic spoken production by two adults with chronic, nonfluent aphasia.

Reciprocal Scaffolding Treatment.   Reciprocal scaffolding treatment (RST) has been described by Avent and Austermann (2003) as based on "an apprenticeship model of learning in which novices learn skills by interacting with a more skilled partner" (p. 397), in a naturalistic communication situation. These authors reported on the successful use of RST by a 65-year old, former physicist with moderate severity of anomic aphasia to teach science lessons to 4- and 5-year old children. In this situation, RST provided the participant with aphasia a meaningful opportunity to use his conceptual knowledge and vocabulary to teach science to young children, thus participating in a valuable societal role. Recently, Avent, Patterson, Lu, and Small (2009) demonstrated successful application of RST, during a seven-week study, by an individual with aphasia who taught novice graduate student clinicians and undergraduate student volunteers how to communicate with persons who have aphasia, during group treatment sessions. It is noteworthy that Avent and her colleagues describe RST as in contrast to conventional treatment techniques where the speech language pathologist is the expert and the person with aphasia is assigned the role of the novice trying to relearn communication skills.

To conclude this section on specific treatment approaches, it is necessary to appreciate that one or more treatment approaches may be combined to enhance treatment outcomes. For example, script training may be enhanced by simple technological applications using real-life videos (Bilda, 2010). Similarly, AAC devices or computer software may be combined with situation-specific therapies such as using voice recognition software to treat writing impairments (Estes & Bloom, 2011). A final important point is that some recent treatment approaches have emerged from combining communication intervention with principles of cognitive rehabilitation and experience-dependent neuroplasticity. For example, the relatively new constraint-induced language treatment (CILT) (Cherney, Patterson, Raymer, Frymark, & Schooling, 2008) combines forced use of verbal language and massed practice to treat communicative impairments in aphasia.

SUMMARY

In summary, persons with aphasia represent a clinically heterogeneous population and it is clear that aphasia manifests differently among affected individuals. Certainly one size cannot fit all when it comes to making decisions about treatment approaches. Clinicians and researchers can choose from a considerable variety of traditional, cognitive neuropsychological or skill-based therapies, technology-based approaches, and life participation approaches to individualize intervention for persons with aphasia. It is essential that there be a working theory for therapy and clear rationale for selecting candidate treatment approaches. In the true spirit of evidence-based practice, this decision making must be based on a thoughtful triangulation of clinician expertise, published evidence, as well as the preferences and priorities of individuals with aphasia.

ACKNOWLEDGMENTS

Preparation of this chapter was supported, in part, by an *Everyday Technologies in Alzheimer Care* (ETAC) grant from the Alzheimer's Association.

REFERENCES

Adult Aphasia and Traumatic Brain Injury Package. (2006). Winooski, VT: Laureate Learning Systems®.

Albert, M., Goodglass, H., Helm, N. A., Rubens, A., & Alexander, M. (1981). *Clinical aspects of dysphasia.* Vienna: Springer.

Albert, M., Sparks, R., & Helm, N. (1973). Melodic intonation therapy for aphasia. *Archives of Neurology, 29*, 130–131.

Alexander, M. P. (1999). D. Frank Benson, M.D.: Contributions to clinical aphasiology. *Aphasiology, 13*(1), 13–20.

Alexander, M. P. (2002). Disorders of language after frontal lobe injury: Evidence for the neural mechanisms of assembling language. In: D. T. Stuss & R. T. Knight (Eds.), *Principles of frontal lobe function* (pp. 292–310). New York: Oxford University Press.

Alexander, M. P., Naeser, M. A., & Palumbo, C. L. (1987). Correlations of subcortical CT lesion sites and aphasia profiles. *Brain, 110*, 961–991.

American Heart Association. (2003). *Stroke facts – all Americans.* Dallas, TX: American Heart Association.

American Speech Language Hearing Association. 2005. *Roles and Responsibilities of Speech-Language Pathologists With Respect to Augmentative and Alternative Communication: Position Statement* [Position Statement]. Available from www.asha.org/policy

Aten, J., Caligiuri, M., & Holland, A. (1982). The efficacy of functional communication therapy for chronic aphasic patients. *Journal of Speech and Hearing Disorders, 47*, 93–96.

Avent, J. (1997). *Manual of cooperative group treatment for aphasia.* Boston, MA: Butterworth-Heinemann.

Avent, J. R., & Austermann, S. (2003). Reciprocal scaffolding: A context for communication treatment in aphasia. *Aphasiology, 17*(4), 397–404.

Avent, J. R., Patterson, J. P., Lu, A., & Small, K. (2009). Reciprocal scaffolding treatment: A person with aphasia as clinical teacher. *Aphasiology, 23*(1), 110–119.

Benson, D. F., & Ardila, A. (1996). *Aphasia: A clinical perspective.* New York: Oxford University Press.

Beeson, P., Antonucci, S., Henry, M., & White, B. (2004). *Anomia, alexia, and agraphia: What you didn't learn in aphasia class.* Presentation, American Speech Language Hearing Association Convention, Philadelphia.

Beeson, P., Bayles, K. A., Rubens, A. B., & Kaszniak, A. (1993). Memory impairments and executive control in individuals with stroke-induced aphasia. *Brain and Language, 45*, 253–275.

Beeson, P., & Hillis, A. (2001). Comprehension and production of written words. In: R. Chapey (Ed.), *Language intervention strategies in aphasia and related neurogenic communication disorders* (4th ed., pp. 572–604). Baltimore, MD: Lippincott Williams & Wilkins.

Beeson, P., Rising, K., Kim, E., & Rapcsak, S. (2010). A treatment sequence for phonological alexia/agraphia. *Journal of Speech Language Hearing Research, 53*, 450–468.

Berthier, M. (1999). *Transcortical aphasias.* Hove, UK: Psychology Press.

Beukelman, D., & Mirenda, P. (2005). *Augmentative and alternative communication: Supporting children and adults with complex communication needs* (3rd ed.). Baltimore, MD: Paul Brookes.

Bhatnagar, S., & Andy, O. (1995). *Neuroscience for the study of communicative disorders.* Baltimore, MD: Williams and Wilkins.

Bilda, K. (2010). Video-based conversational script training for aphasia: A therapy study. *Aphasiology, iFirst*, 1–11.

Bollinger, R., Musson, N., & Holland, A. (1993). A study of group communication intervention with chronically aphasic persons. *Aphasiology, 7*, 301–313.

Boyle, M. (2001). Semantic feature analysis: The evidence for treating lexical impairments. *Neurophysiology and Neurogenic Speech and Language Disorders, 11*, 23–28.

Boyle, M., & Coelho, C. (1995). Application of semantic feature analysis as a treatment for aphasic dysnomia. *American Journal of Speech-Language Pathology, 4*, 94–98.

Brookshire, N. (2007). Right hemisphere syndrome. In: *Introduction to neurogenic communication disorders* (7th ed., pp. 391–444). St. Louis, MO: Mosby Inc.

Bungalow Software© (1995–2006). Retrieved from http://www.bungalowsoftware.com. Accessed on December 15, 2006.

Burgio, F., & Basso, A. (1997). Memory and aphasia. *Neuropsychologia, 35*, 759–766.

Buzolich, M. (2006). Augmentative and alternative communication (AAC) assessment: Adult aphasia. *Neurophysiology and Neurogenic Speech and Language Disorders, 16*(4), 4–12.

Chapey, R. (2001). *Language intervention strategies in aphasia and related neurogenic communication disorders* (4th ed.). Baltimore, MD: Lippincott Williams and Wilkins.

Cherney, L. R., Patterson, J. P., Raymer, A., Frymark, T., & Schooling, T. (2008). Evidence-based systematic review: Effects of intensity of treatment and constraint-induced language therapy for individuals with stroke-induced aphasia. *Journal of Speech Language Hearing Research, 51*, 1282–1299.

Coelho, C. A., McHugh, R. E., & Boyle, M. (2000). Semantic feature analysis as a treatment for aphasic dysnomia: A replication. *Aphasiology, 14*(2), 133–142.

Coppens, P., Hungerford, S., Yamaguchi, S., & Yamadori, A. (2002). Crossed aphasia: An analysis of the symptoms, their frequency, and a comparison with left hemisphere aphasia symptomatology. *Brain & Language, 83*, 425–463.

Damasio, A. R. (1998). Signs of aphasia. In: M. T. Sarno (Ed.), *Acquired aphasia* (pp. 25–40). New York: Academic Press.

Damasio, H. (1991). Neuroanatomical correlates of the aphasias. In: M. T. Sarno (Ed.), *Acquired aphasia* (2nd ed.). New York: Academic Press.

Damasio, H. (2001). Neural basis of language disorders. In: R. Chapey (Ed.), *Language intervention strategies in adult aphasia* (ed., pp. 18–36). Baltimore, MD: Lippincott Williams & Wilkins.

Damasio, H., & Damasio, A. R. (1980). The anatomical basis of conduction aphasia. *Brain, 103*, 337–350.

Darley, F. L., Aronson, A. E., & Brown, J. R. (1975). *Motor speech disorders*. Toronto, Canada: W. B. Saunders.

Davis, G. A. (2000). *Aphasiology: Disorders and clinical practice* (1st ed.). Boston, MA: Pearson Education.

Davis, G. A. (2005). PACE revisited. *Aphasiology, 19*, 21–38.

Davis, G. A. (2007). *Aphasiology: Disorders and clinical practice* (2nd ed.). Boston, MA: Pearson Education.

Davis, G. A., & Wilcox, M. J. (1981). Incorporating parameters of natural conversation in aphasia treatment. In: R. Chapey (Ed.), *Language intervention strategies in adult aphasia* (pp. 169–193). Baltimore, MD: Lippincott Williams & Wilkins.

Davis, G. A., & Wilcox, M. J. (1985). *Adult aphasia rehabilitation: Applied pragmatics*. San Diego, CA: Singular Publishing Group.

Dronkers, N. F. (1993). *Cerebral localization of production deficits in aphasia.* Telerounds No. 9. Tucson, AZ: National Center for Neurogenic Communication Disorders.

Dronkers, N. F. (1996). A new brain region for coordinating speech articulation. *Nature, 384,* 159–161.

Dronkers, N. F., Shapiro, J. K., Redfern, B. B., & Knight, J. K. (1992). The role of Broca's area in Broca's aphasia. *Journal of Clinical and Experimental Neuropsychology, 14,* 52–53.

Duffy, J. R. (2005). *Motor speech disorders: Substrates, differential diagnosis, and management* (2nd ed.). St Louis, MO: Elsevier Mosby.

Duffy, J. R., & Coelho, C. A. (2001). Schuell's stimulation approach to rehabilitation. In: R. Chapey (Ed.), *Language intervention strategies in adult Aphasia* (4th ed., pp. 341–382). Baltimore, MD: Lippincott Williams & Wilkins.

Elman, R. J. (2005). Social and life participation approaches to aphasia intervention. In: L. L. LaPointe (Ed.), *Aphasia and related neurogenic language disorders* (3rd ed., pp. 39–50). New York: Thieme Publishers.

Elman, R. J. (2006). *Group treatment of neurogenic communication disorders: The expert clinician's approach.* San Diego, CA: Plural Publishing.

Estes, C., & Bloom, R. L. (2011). Using voice recognition software to treat dysgraphia in a patient with conduction aphasia. *Aphasiology, 25*(3), 366–385.

Ferstl, E. C., Guthke, T., & von Cramon, D. Y. (1999). Change of perspective in discourse comprehension: Encoding and retrieval processes after brain injury. *Brain and Language, 70,* 385–420.

Frattali, C., & Grafman, J. (2005). Language and discourse deficits following prefrontal cortex damage. In: L. L. LaPointe (Ed.), *Aphasia and related neurogenic language disorders* (3rd ed., pp. 51–67). New York: Thieme Publishers.

Gabrieli, J. D., Poldrack, R. A., & Desmond, J. E. (1998). The role of the left prefrontal cortex in language and memory. *Proceedings of the National Academy of Sciences, 95,* 906–913.

Geschwind, N. (1965). Disconnection syndromes in animals and man. *Brain, 88,* 237–294.

Goodglass, H., & Kaplan, E. (1972). *The Boston diagnostic aphasia examination.* Philadelphia: Lea & Febiger.

Goodglass, H., Kaplan, E., & Barresi, B. (2001). *The assessment of aphasia and related disorders* (3rd ed.). Baltimore, MD: Lippincott, Williams & Wilkins.

Grabowski, T. J., & Damasio, A. R. (2004). Definition, clinical features, and neuroanatomical basis of dementia. In: M. Esiri, V. Lee & J. Trojanowski (Eds.), *Neuropathology of dementia* (2nd ed., pp. 1–10). Cambridge, UK: Cambridge University Press.

Hartley, L. L. (1995). *Cognitive-communicative abilities following brain injury: A functional approach.* San Diego, CA: Singular Publishing Group.

Haynes, W. O., & Pindzola, R. H. (2004). Assessment of aphasia and adult language disorders. In: *Diagnosis and evaluation in speech pathology* (6th ed., pp. 219–243). Boston, MA: Pearson Education.

Helm-Estabrooks, N., & Albert, M. (2004a). Neuropathology of aphasia. In: *Manual of aphasia and aphasia therapy* (2nd ed., pp. 17–30). Austin, TX: Pro-Ed Publishers.

Helm-Estabrooks, N., & Albert, M. (2004b). Melodic intonation therapy. In: *Manual of aphasia and aphasia therapy* (2nd ed., pp. 221–233). Austin, TX: Pro-Ed Publishers.

Helm-Estabrooks, N., Fitzpatrick, P., & Barresi, B. (1982). Visual action therapy for global aphasia. *Journal of Speech and Hearing Disorders, 47,* 385–389.

Hillis, A. E. (2001). Cognitive neuropsychological approaches to rehabilitation of language disorders: Introduction. In: R. Chapey (Ed.), *Language intervention strategies in adult aphasia* (4th ed., pp. 513–521). Baltimore, MD: Lippincott Williams & Wilkins.

Ho, K. M., Weiss, S. J., Garrett, K., & Lloyd, L. (2005). The effect of remnant and pictographic books on the communicative interaction of individuals with global aphasia. *Augmentative and Alternative Communication, 21*, 218–232.

Holland, A., & Beeson, P. (1999). Aphasia groups: The Arizona experience. In: R. J. Elman (Ed.), *Group treatment of neurogenic communication disorders: The expert clinician's approach* (pp. 77–84). Boston, MA: Butterworth Heinemann.

Hopper, T. (2001). Indirect interventions to facilitate communication in Alzheimer's disease. *Seminars in Speech and Language, 22*(4), 305–315.

Hopper, T., & Holland, A. (1998). Situation-specific training for adults with aphasia: An example. *Aphasiology, 12*(10), 933–944.

Hopper, T., Holland, A., & Rewega, M. (2002). Conversational coaching: Treatment outcomes and future directions. *Aphasiology, 16*(7), 745–761.

Kertesz, A. B. (2007). *Western aphasia battery-revised*. San Antonio, TX: Pearson.

Kiran, S. (2006). Pure alexia: Causes, characteristics, and treatment. *Neurophysiology and Neurogenic Speech and Language Disorders, 16*(1), 16–20.

Klein, E. R., & Mancinelli, J. M. (2010). *Acquired language disorders: A case-based approach*. San Diego, CA: Plural Publishing.

Koul, R., Petroi, D., & Schlosser, R. (2010). Systematic review of speech generating devices for aphasia. In: S. Stern & J. W. Mullennix (Eds.), *Computer synthesized speech technologies: Tools for aiding impairment* (pp. 148–160). Hershey, PA: IGI Global.

Koul, R. K., & Corwin, M. (2003). Efficacy of AAC intervention in chronic severe aphasia. In: R. W. Schlosser, H. H. Arvidson & L. L. Lloyd (Eds.), *The efficacy of augmentative and alternative communication: Toward evidence-based practice* (pp. 449–470). San Diego, CA: Academic Press.

LaPointe, L. L. (1985). Aphasia therapy: Some principles and strategies for treatment. In: D. F. Johns (Ed.), *Clinical management of neurogenic communicative disorders* (pp. 179–241). Boston, MA: Little Brown.

Laures, J., Odell, K. H., & Coe, L. (2003). Arousal and auditory vigilance in individuals with aphasia during a linguistic and nonlinguistic task. *Aphasiology, 17*(12), 1133–1152.

Logemann, J. (1997). *Evaluation and treatment of swallowing disorders* (2nd ed.). Austin, TX: ProEd Publishers.

Love, R. J., & Webb, W. G. (1996). The central language mechanism and its disorders. In: *Neurology for the speech language pathologist* (3rd ed., pp. 195–255). Boston, MA: Butterworth-Heinemann.

Lowell, S., Beeson, P. M., & Holland, A. (1995). The efficacy of a semantic cueing procedure on naming performance of adults with aphasia. *American Journal of Speech Language Pathology, 4*(4), 109–114.

Lyon, J., & Shadden, B. B. (2001). Treating life consequences of aphasia's chronicity. In: R. Chapey (Ed.), *Language intervention strategies in adult aphasia* (4th ed.). Baltimore, MD: Lippincott Williams & Wilkins.

Lyon, J. G., Cariski, D., Keisler, L., Rosenbek, J., Levine, R., Kumpula, J., ... Blanc, M. (1997). Communication partners: Enhancing participation in life and communication for adults with aphasia in natural settings. *Aphasiology*, *11*(7), 693–708.

Lytton, R. (2005). *Update on augmentative and alternative communication: Forum on clinical hot topics in health care*. Presentation, American Speech Language Hearing Convention, San Diego.

Mahendra, N. (2001). Direct interventions for improving the performance of individuals with Alzheimer's disease. *Seminars in Speech and Language*, *22*(4), 289–302.

Martino, R., Foley, N., Bhogal, S., Diamant, N., Speechley, M., & Teasell, R. (2005). Dysphagia after stroke: Incidence, diagnosis, and pulmonary complications. *Stroke*, *36*, 2756–2763.

Mayer, J. F., Turkstra, L., Murray, L., & Lorenzen, B. (2006). *The nature of working memory deficits in aphasia*. Presentation, American Speech Language Hearing Convention, Miami Beach.

McNeil, M. R., & Duffy, J. R. (2001). Primary progressive aphasia. In: R. Chapey (Ed.), *Language intervention strategies in adult aphasia* (4th ed.). Baltimore, MD: Lippincott Williams & Wilkins.

Mesulam, M. M. (1982). Slowly progressive aphasia without dementia. *Annals of Neurology*, *11*, 592–598.

Mesulam, M. M. (2000). Behavioral neuroanatomy: Large scale networks, association cortex, frontal syndromes, the limbic system, and hemispheric specialization. In: *Principles of behavioral and cognitive neurology* (2nd ed., pp. 41–48). New York: Oxford University Press.

Mesulam, M. M. (2006). *Behavioral biology of primary progressive aphasia (PPA)*. Paper presented at the Fifth International Conference on Frontotemporal Dementias, San Francisco, CA, USA.

Miller, N. (2002). The neurological bases for apraxia of speech. *Seminars in Speech and Language*, *23*(4), 223–230.

Murray, L. L. (2002). Attention deficits in aphasia: presence, nature, assessment, and treatment. *Seminars in Speech and Language*, *23*(2), 107–116.

Murray, L. L., & Clark, H. M. (2006). Assessment of function: Quantifying and qualifying linguistic disorders. In: *Neurogenic disorders of language: Theory-driven clinical practice* (pp. 123–176). Clifton, NY: Thomson Delmar Learning.

Myers, P. S. (2001). Toward a definition of RHD syndrome. *Aphasiology*, *15*(10/11), 913–918.

National Institute of Neurological Disorders and Stroke (August 2002). *Post-stroke rehabilitation fact sheet* (NIH Publication No. 02-4846). Bethesda, MD: Author.

National Institute on Deafness and Other Communication Disorders. (2006). *Statistics on voice, speech and language*. Retrieved from http://www.nidcd.nih.gov/health/statistics/vsl.asp#3. Accessed on December 4.

National Stroke Association. (June 2006). *Stroke facts*. Retrieved from http://www.stroke.org/site/DocServer/Stroke_Fact_Sheet_with_Graphics_6.26.06.pdf?docID=1944

O'Connor, B., Anema, I., Datta, H., Signorelli, T., & Obler, L. K. (2005). Agrammatism: A cross-linguistic clinical perspective. *The ASHA Leader*, December 27.

Paghera, B., Marien, P., & Vignolo, L. A. (2003). Crossed aphasia with left spatial neglect and visual imperception: A case report. *Neurological Science*, *23*, 317–322.

Parrot Software© (1981–2007). Retrieved from http://www.parrotsoftware.com. Accessed on January 1, 2007.

Patterson, K. E., & Shewell, C. (1987). Speak and spell: Dissociations and word class effects. In: M. Coltheart, J. Rob & G. Sartori (Eds.), *The cognitive neuropsychology of language.* Hillsdale, NJ: Lawrence Erlbaum.

Rider, J. D., Wright, H. H., Marshall, R. C., & Page, J. L. (2008). Using semantic feature analysis to improve contextual discourse in adults with aphasia. *American Journal of Speech Language Pathology, 17,* 161–172.

Schwartz, M. F., Saffran, E. M., Fink, R. B., Myers, J. L., & Martin, N. (1994). Mapping therapy: A treatment programme for agrammatism. *Aphasiology, 8,* 19–54.

Shapiro, L. P. (1997). Tutorial: An introduction to syntax. *Journal of Speech Language and Hearing Research, 40,* 254–272.

Sheehy, L. M. (2006). Crossed aphasia: A review of the syndrome. *Neurophysiology and Neurogenic Speech and Language Disorders, 16*(1), 11–16.

Simmons-Mackie, N. (2001). Social participation approaches to aphasia intervention. In: R. Chapey (Ed.), *Language intervention strategies in adult aphasia* (4th ed., pp. 246–266). Baltimore, MD: Lippincott Williams & Wilkins.

Sparks, R. W. (2001). Melodic intonation therapy. In: R. Chapey (Ed.), *Language intervention strategies in adult aphasia* (4th ed., pp. 703–717). Baltimore, MD: Lippincott Williams & Wilkins.

TheraSimplicity™ Software Library (©1997–2007). Retrieved from http://www.therasimplicity .com/Home.aspx. Accessed on December 22, 2006.

Thompson, C. K. (2001). Treatment of underlying forms: A linguistic specific approach for sentence production deficits in agrammatic aphasia. In: R. Chapey (Ed.), *Language intervention strategies in adult aphasia* (4th ed., pp. 605–628). Baltimore, MD: Lippincott Williams & Wilkins.

Whitworth, A., Webster, J., & Howard, D. (2005). Introduction to therapy. In: *A cognitive neuropsychological approach to assessment and intervention in aphasia: A clinician's guide* (pp. 107–114). New York: Psychology Press.

Williams, G. R., Jiang, J. G., Matchar, D. B., & Samsa, G. P. (1999). Incidence and occurrence of total (first-ever and recurrent) stroke. *Stroke, 30,* 2523–2528.

World Health Organization. (2001). *International classification of functioning, disability, and health, ICF.* Geneva, Switzerland: WHO.

Wright, H. H., Newhoff, M., Downey, R., & Austermann, S. (2003). Additional data on working memory in aphasia. *Journal of International Neuropsychological Society, 9,* 302.

Wright, H. H., & Shisler, R. J. (2005). Working memory in aphasia: Theory, measures, and clinical applications. *American Journal of Speech Language Pathology, 14*(2), 107–118.

Youmans, G., Holland, A., Munoz, M., & Bourgeois, M. (2010). Script training and automaticity in two individuals with aphasia. *Aphasiology, 19*(3), 435–450.

CHAPTER 3

OVERVIEW OF AAC INTERVENTION APPROACHES FOR PERSONS WITH APHASIA

Rajinder Koul

INTRODUCTION

Aphasia is a language impairment resulting from damage to areas of the brain that are responsible for the comprehension and formulation of language. Speech and language treatment approaches to remediate language impairment in persons with aphasia (PWA) have evolved over the past century. The catalytic event that enhanced the role of behavioral intervention in aphasia rehabilitation was the presence of a large number of World War II veterans who had acquired aphasia after traumatic brain injuries (Benson & Ardilla, 1996). Since that time, there has been continuous advancement in the development of medical and behavioral intervention approaches for PWA. This advancement was primarily a result of the following factors: (1) development of imaging technology such as functional magnetic resonance imaging, positron emission tomography, and computerized tomography that has enhanced understanding of brain organization of language; (2) increase in knowledge base in neurophysiology and neural mechanisms that underlie recovery after brain-injury; (3) increase in empirical data that provide strong scientific basis for the wide spectrum of

Augmentative and Alternative Communication for Adults with Aphasia
Augmentative and Alternative Communications Perspectives, Volume 3, 47–63
Copyright © 2011 by Emerald Group Publishing Limited
ISSN: 2047-0991/doi:10.1108/S2047-0991(2011)0000003009

language and other behavioral intervention approaches; and (4) advances in computer technology and speech synthesis resulting in the development of software programs and speech generating devices (SGDs) that have provided new avenues of communication for PWA (Koul & Corwin, 2003).

There is a wide variability in linguistic characteristics demonstrated by PWA (e.g., Brookshire, 2003; Goodglass & Kaplan, 1983; Kertesz, 1982; Porch, 1981). The linguistic characteristics and associated sensori-motor symptoms observed in PWA depend on several factors such as the size of the lesion, the role of the damaged locus in processing the specific brain function, and the remote effects of the lesion on distant brain tissue (Mountcastle, 1978). These factors in conjunction with socio-demographic variables (e.g., age, gender, education) play a strong role in the recovery of language function in PWA. Many PWA demonstrate severe speech and language deficits, and their ability to use natural language may be permanently and severely impaired (Koul & Corwin, 2003). Such individuals may benefit from augmentative and alternative communication (AAC) methods. These include symbols, aids, techniques, and strategies for either augmenting speech and/or providing an alternative means of communication (Lloyd, Fuller, & Arvidson, 1997). The primary purpose of this chapter is to provide a comprehensive review of approaches to classify AAC for PWA. Two approaches to AAC intervention will be presented. The first approach relates to the presence or absence of the use of technology in AAC intervention (Koul & Corwin, 2003). This approach proposes that all components of AAC systems (i.e., symbols, aids, techniques, strategies, and partner education/training) must be integrated to produce desired results. The second approach focuses on the communication needs, cognitive-linguistic competencies, and participation levels of PWA (Garrett & Lasker, 2005; Lasker, Garret, & Fox, 2007). This approach proposes that candidates for AAC intervention can be classified into two primary clinical groups: partner-dependent communicators and partner-independent communicators. Within these two primary groups are several subgroups based primarily on specific cognitive-linguistic competencies of PWA.

AAC INTERVENTION BASED ON USE OF TECHNOLOGY OR NO-TECHNOLOGY OPTIONS

This section provides a comprehensive review of the two major AAC options available for PWA.

Technology-Based AAC Intervention Approaches

This section provides an overview of technology-based AAC approaches currently available to PWA. For the purposes of this text, technology-based approaches include the use of dedicated SGDs and/or software programs and applications that turn computers or hand-held electronic devices into communication devices that produce digitized or synthesized speech output upon selection of messages.

Owing to rapid advances in computer technology, AAC aids such as SGDs and software programs for hand-held multipurpose electronic devices (e.g., iPod, iPad) have become increasingly available to PWA (Koul, Petroi, & Schlosser, 2010). Most dedicated SGDs, software programs, and applications (e.g., DynaVox V™ & Vmax™ by DynaVox®, SpeechPRO software by Gus Communications Inc., SmallTalk by Lingraphica® Company, and Vanguard Plus by PRC) are not disorder specific. These devices/software programs are designed, as well as promoted, to be used by persons with speech and language impairment, irrespective of the cause of the impairment. There is, however, one commercially available SGD (i.e., Lingraphica® by Lingraphica®: The Aphasia Company™) that is specifically designed and promoted for use by PWA.

One of the most challenging aspects, both conceptually and technologically, is the manner in which vocabulary/messages are organized in SGDs so that they can be easily retrieved by AAC users. Most of the commercially available SGDs provide options that allow the AAC user to access messages from grid displays. There are three types of grid displays: taxonomic, semantic-syntactic, and visual-scene (Beukelman & Mirenda, 2005). The taxonomic display is the most frequently used vocabulary organization option in research studies that have investigated the effectiveness of AAC intervention in PWA (e.g., Koul, Corwin, & Hayes, 2005; Koul, Corwin, Nigam, & Oetzel, 2008; Rostron, Ward, & Plant, 1996). The taxonomic grid display provides for the presentation of symbols across multiple screens in a logical sequence. The AAC user may select one of the superordinate categories (e.g., sports) on the first screen. This will bring up a second screen with several subordinate categories (e.g., football, basketball, cricket). Selecting "cricket" on the second screen will bring up the third screen with subordinate categories for the national teams (e.g., England, Australia, India). The screens are designed so that each symbol/message is displayed on a separate grid with an option to produce a spoken message upon selection of a symbol. Figs. 1–3 provide a depiction of a taxonomic grid display. Fig. 1 depicts a "supermarket" screen in which the AAC user can

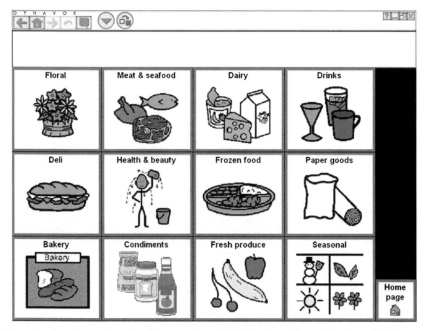

Fig. 1. An Example of a Taxonomic Grid Display Menu Developed Using a
DynaVox® SGD.

choose from various supermarket departments (e.g., bakery, deli, condiments). If "Condiments" is selected, the next screen the AAC user will see is
Fig. 2. The screen depicted by Fig. 2 allows the AAC user to choose a
condiment (e.g., ketchup, salt, pepper) of their choice. Fig. 3 depicts a "main
menu" screen with various options for the AAC user. Examples include a
photo album, appliances, and questions. Selection of any of these categories
will lead the AAC user to a new screen. Results from studies that have used
a taxonomic grid display indicate that persons with severe chronic aphasia
are able to access, manipulate, and combine symbols across several screens
to produce simple sentences and phrases (Koul et al., 2005, 2008; Koul &
Harding, 1998).

The semantic-syntactic grid display option organizes vocabulary based on
a syntactical framework, such as sentence word order. It is considered
primarily for children with developmental speech and language impairments
(Beukelman & Mirenda, 2005). Vocabulary is organized from left to right
across the display to allow for sentence construction. Review of published

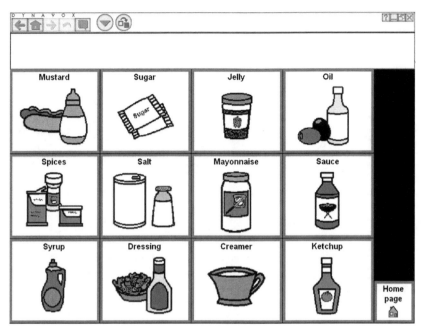

Fig. 2. Taxonomic Grid Display Screen Featuring Various Condiments Accessed
by Selecting "Condiments" from the Previous Screen.

research on AAC and aphasia indicates that this display has not been used
to investigate the effectiveness of AAC intervention for PWA (Fitzgerald,
1976). This is understandable given the fact that most persons with Broca's
and global aphasia demonstrate severe syntactic deficits including absence
of function words and grammatical markers in their speech.

The visual scene display option is an option for organizing messages that
provides both personalization and greater context for communication
between AAC users and their communication partners (Beukelman &
Mirenda, 2005; McKelvey, Dietz, Hux, Weissling, & Beukelman, 2007).
This option provides for organization of vocabulary related to activities,
schemes, or routines (e.g., vocabulary related to an activity such as watching
a soccer game). Each display contains symbols representing vocabulary
elements (e.g., people, descriptors, feelings) that are related to an activity
and are organized schematically. This option also allows for downloading
personal photographs and other pictures and creating virtual environments.
For example, a virtual environment can depict a scene showing an AAC

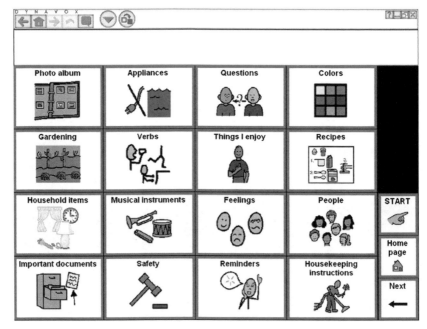

Fig. 3. Example of a Taxonomic Grid Display Menu Developed Using a DynaVox® SGD Featuring Various Superordinate Categories.

user's kitchen with a stove, refrigerator, oven, cabinets, sink, and a dining table (Fig. 4). Selecting the refrigerator will result in the refrigerator opening to reveal the food items inside. Review of studies that have used visual scene displays with PWA indicates its potential in facilitating communication in PWA (e.g., McKelvey et al., 2007).

No-Technology-Based AAC Intervention Approaches

Although several classification systems have been developed to distinguish between various types of assistive technologies (Wasson, Arvidson & Lloyd, 1997), this text uses the technology/no-technology dichotomy in which no-technology-based intervention approaches do not involve production of speech output upon selection of a message. Communication books/boards, cue cards, and memory books are examples of no-technology approaches. A number of studies have been conducted in which AAC intervention involved the use of alphabet cards, photographs, graphic symbols, written

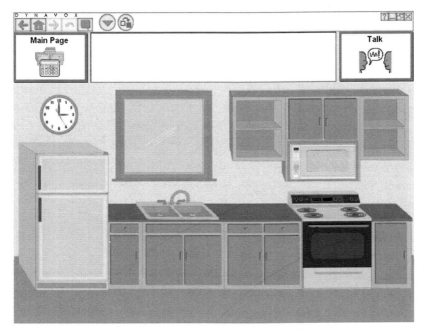

Fig. 4. Visual Scene Display of a Kitchen from a DynaVox® SGD.

choices, gestures, drawing, writing, communication boards, or remnant books (e.g., Fox, Sohlberg, Fried-Oken, 2001; Lasker, Hux, Garret, Moncrief, & Eischied, 1997; Ward-Lonergan & Nicholas, 1995). Results of these studies indicate that PWA are able to use various no-technology options with varying degrees of success.

AAC INTERVENTION BASED ON COMMUNICATION NEEDS, COMPETENCIES, AND PARTICIPATION LEVELS

Garret and Beukelman (1992) proposed a novel classification system that took into consideration needs, cognitive-linguistic competencies, and participation levels of persons with severe aphasia. The classification system was revised in 2005 with the aim of facilitating selection of appropriate AAC intervention strategies, techniques, and aids for persons with specific communication needs (Garrett and Lasker, 2005). According to this classification, PWA are classified into two broad categories: partner-dependent and partner-independent communicators.

Partner-Dependent Communicators

Garret and Beukelman (1995, 1998) and Kagan (1998) observed that some PWA may always remain dependent on communication partners in initiating communication interactions and managing informational demands. These PWA are referred to as partner-dependent and are further subcategorized into three types: emerging communicators, contextual choice communicators, and transitional communicators.

Emerging Communicators

Emerging communicators were previously referred to as basic-choice communicators (Garret & Beukelman, 1992). These communicators primarily depict characteristics of persons with global aphasia. They demonstrate severe deficits in all aspects of language (i.e., spontaneous speech, auditory comprehension, reading and writing). Many speech-language pathologists evaluate and treat these patients while they are in either acute care settings or after they have been discharged to long-term care facilities or their own homes (Garrett & Lasker, 2005). These individuals may also have difficulties processing information as well as maintaining attention. Garrett and Lasker (2005) recommended that intervention goals and strategies for emerging communicators should primarily focus on choice-making and accurately signaling affirmation for preferred items and rejection for nonpreferred items. Additionally, turn taking in familiar contexts and partner training are critical to successful intervention. Partners must be given instruction related to utilizing augmented input strategies, providing choice-making opportunities, and reinforcing accurate responses. Emerging communicators have the potential to benefit from no-technology approaches that use photographs, line drawings, and pictures to communicate basic needs and wants related to activities of daily living. They are also able to participate in familiar social activities, if they are provided with symbols, strategies, and trained communication partners who are able to provide appropriate cues and feedback. An example of an AAC intervention using pictures of items with an emerging communicator follows:

Communication Partner: "Do you want to eat a snack or get something to drink?"

AAC User: [Points to Drink]
Communication Partner: "Do you want milk or juice?

AAC User: [Points to Milk]
Communication Partner: [Pours milk into glass]

Contextual-Choice Communicators
The contextual-choice communicators were previously referred to as controlled-situation communicators (Garret & Beukelman, 1992). These communicators are able to identify photographs and line drawings and can spontaneously point to objects and/or symbols to communicate basic wants and needs. Garrett and Lasker (2005) observed that many contextual-choice communicators do not initiate conversation and thus are socially isolated.

Persons with chronic severe Broca's aphasia, severe Wernicke's aphasia, and transcortical motor aphasia generally fall into the category of contextual-choice communicators. AAC intervention goals and strategies for contextual-choice communicators include a written choice conversation technique in which keywords are provided by the partner. AAC users point to the words to make their preferences or opinions known. Additionally, contextual-choice communicators can use scales or maps to talk about quantifying events or locations (Garrett & Lasker, 2005). They can also use alternative modes such as gestures, drawing, and writing to communicate with others. If contextual-choice communicators have severe deficits in auditory comprehension, communication partners must be given instruction on augmented input techniques. The partners must write or draw keywords, gesture, and/or point to items being discussed if it appears that the PWA is unable to completely or partially understand auditory information (Lasker et al., 2007). An example of an interaction using a written-choice conversation follows:

Communication Partner: "What did you eat for lunch yesterday?"
[Writes in large block letters while simultaneously saying:
{CHICKEN "Chicken"
STEAK "Steak"
PEANUT BUTTER AND CRACKERS "Peanut butter and crackers"
TURKEY SANDWICH "Turkey sandwich"}]
AAC User: [Points to TURKEY SANDWICH]
Communication Partner: "Oh that sounds delicious! Who made the turkey sandwich?"
[Writes in large block letters while simultaneously saying:
{DAUGHTER "Daughter"
SON "Son"
HUSBAND "Husband"}]
AAC User: [Points to DAUGHTER]
Communication Partner: "What did you have on your turkey sandwich?"
[Writes in large block letters while simultaneously saying:
{MAYO "Mayo"
MUSTARD "Mustard"
NONE OF THE ABOVE "None of the above"}]
AAC User: [Points to MUSTARD]
Communication Partner: "I love mustard on my turkey sandwiches. What did you drink with your turkey sandwich?" [Writes in large block letters while simultaneously saying:
{SPRITE "Sprite"

COCA-COLA "Coca-Cola"
WATER "Water"
ICED TEA "Iced tea"}]
AAC User: [Points to ICED TEA]
Communication Partner: "That sounds like a great lunch!"
AAC User: [Nods head]

Transitional Communicators
Transitional communicators are able to point to symbols or words and can use gestures to augment their spoken language. This category represents PWA who are progressing toward being independent communicators with the capability to generate novel and stored messages without any partner support (Garrett & Lasker, 2005). However, a transitional communicator depends on cues and prompts to answer questions and stay engaged in a spontaneous conversation. AAC intervention goals and strategies for transitional communicators may include use of either high-technology AAC options (e.g., SGDs) or no-technology options (e.g., communication books or boards) to communicate in commonly occurring situations such as ordering food in a cafeteria or answering predictable questions using pre-stored messages on an SGD. An example of an interaction using prestored messages on an SGD is as follows:

Communication Partner: "Mine, I like chicken fajitas."
AAC User: "Oh, yes." [Activates SGD prerecorded message: *"I want to eat at the steak place."*]
Communication Partner: "Oh, that's the restaurant."
AAC User: "Yes, oh no."
Communication Partner: "They have some good food there too. I like Gomez."
AAC User: "Oh, yes."
Communication Partner: "Uh-huh."
AAC User: "Oh."
Communication Partner: "They got some good food there huh?"
AAC User: "Oh yes, thank you." [Activates SGD prerecorded message: *"I like spaghetti."*]
Communication Partner: "Mmm-hmm."
AAC User: "Oh no, thank you."
Communication Partner: "I like spaghetti."
AAC User: "Oh no, yes, thank you, oh, thank you, yes." [Activates SGD prerecorded message: *"I like pizza with mushrooms and olives."*]

Communication Partner: "Oh yes, now that's some good pizza there."
AAC User: "Yes."
Communication Partner: "Olives, I mean mushrooms."
AAC User: "Yes, oh yes, thank you, thank you."
Communication Partner: "I like mushrooms."
AAC User: "Oh thank you, yes, yes, yes, yes."
Communication Partner: "I know you like guacamole."

Partner-Independent Communicators

Partner-independent communicators are individuals who have severe expressive speech and language deficits. However, their comprehension is relatively adequate, and they require little to no contextual support to aid auditory comprehension (Garrett & Lasker, 2005). Independent communicators may depict characteristics of persons with moderate to severe Broca's aphasia, transcortical motor aphasia, or conduction aphasia. Independent communicators are further subclassified into three types: stored-message communicators, generative-message communicators, and specific-need communicators.

Stored-Message Communicators

Stored-message communicators are independently able to use AAC systems to supplement their speech (Garrett & Lasker, 2005; Lasker & Bedrosian, 2001). AAC intervention strategies for stored-message communicators include the retrieval and use of messages stored in the SGDs in familiar communicative situations such as selecting a cell phone from various cell phones at a store. These individuals may also be able to access, identify, and manipulate symbols and messages displayed across several screens on an SGD. However, their ability to use an SGD to communicate novel information in unfamiliar contexts is generally limited. Stored-message communicators require practice in efficiently identifying and selecting vocabulary so that they become able to communicate in a variety of situations. Clinicians must involve both stored-message communicators and their family members when they develop the inventory of messages to be programmed in SGDs and displayed in communication books and wallets. Decisions regarding whether to use a no-technology or a high-technology AAC system should be made only after evaluating advantages and disadvantages of each system and doing a trial run with a high-technology system before recommending it. An example interaction with a stored-message communicator using a visual scene display follows:

AAC User: [Taps on volunteer's shoulder]
Volunteer: "Hi!"
AAC User: [Activates SGD: *"Would you like to see my family?"*]
Volunteer: "What is that you're using?"
AAC User: [Goes to main menu and activates SGD: *"I had a stroke 3 years ago. This device helps me communicate."*]
Volunteer: "Oh okay, what is your name?"
AAC User: "Tuze ... tuze ..." [Activates SGD: *"My name is Susan Smith."*]
Volunteer: "It's nice to meet you Susan. Were you going to show me your family?"
AAC User: "Faly" [Returns to Family level on SGD: *"Our family."*]
Volunteer: "Wow, you have a beautiful family!"

Generative-Message Communicators
Generative-message communicators are able to communicate independently in multiple settings using either limited speech and/or writing (Garrett & Lasker, 2005). These individuals were previously referred to as comprehensive communicators who wish to participate in various communicative situations (Garret & Beukelman, 1992). However, their ability to communicate novel information is either fragmented or inconsistent resulting in communication breakdowns (Garrett & Lasker, 2005). AAC intervention techniques for generative-message communicators include identifying their participatory patterns and communication needs and providing them with various AAC techniques that they can use to facilitate their communication. Many generative-message communicators have the potential to use high-technology AAC systems that employ features such as visual scene displays or software programs that allow them to participate in small talk by accessing communication messages stored by pragmatic functions such as greetings (Todman & Alm, 2003). The critical aspect of AAC intervention with generative-message communicators is that they need substantial instruction as well as practice in AAC strategies and techniques that have been recommended for them. An example of interaction using a combination of words, symbols, and letters on an SGD follows:

Mrs. B was a retired school teacher with moderate expressive aphasia and good comprehension. She learned to use a portable SGD in combination with words, symbols, and letters. Mrs. B lived with her husband, but she maintained independence in many aspects of her life (e.g., she continued to drive herself, enjoyed gardening, and cooked and baked often). Mrs. B used residual speech along with drawing and writing to communicate in most situations. She used an SGD to supplement her speech, particularly around those people with whom she rarely or never spoke on a regular basis (e.g., grocery store clerk). Mrs. B used her SGD to spell out short words or the first few letters of long words. She used various stored phrases when rapid communication was needed (e.g., "*No thank you*"). She combined her residual speech, writing, and SGD to communicate in various contexts.

Specific-Need Communicators
Persons with mild aphasia who have difficulty in specific situations because of clarity and specificity of information required in those situations fall under the category of specific-need communicators (Garret & Beukelman, 1992; Garrett & Lasker, 2005). These individuals may not need AAC or do not wish to use AAC but do need communication support in certain situations. Many of these individuals have a severe word-finding disability that may cause a lack of specificity and clarity when communicating with

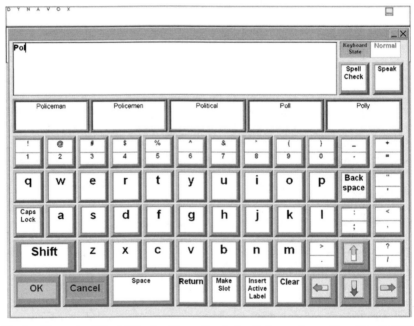

Fig. 5.   Example of Single Word or Phrase Prediction Software from a DynaVox® SGD.

others (Garrett & Lasker, 2005). AAC intervention strategies for these individuals include analyzing the requirements of specific communication tasks and providing strategies and techniques that can help AAC users communicate with relatively greater clarity. For example, a lady with severe anomia may use word or phrase prediction software (Fig. 5) to support her writing. A communication card with specific instructions about buying a dress can help reduce communication breakdowns. An example interaction using word prediction software follows:

AAC User: "I want to go to the movies t... "
AAC User types letter t into SGD word prediction software and the following words appear:

1. to	2. take	3. too
4. time	5. tell	6. turn

AAC User types *to* into SGD word prediction software:

1. to	2. too	3. today
4. tonight	5. tomorrow	6. told

AAC User chooses tonight to finish her sentence – "I want to go to the movies tonight."

CONCLUSIONS

The success of AAC intervention in PWA depends on not only carefully matching capabilities of PWA to specific AAC strategies and techniques but also training primary communication partners to use communication strategies that can facilitate communication of PWA. It is also critical that AAC intervention be dynamic so that appropriate strategies are in place as PWA make a transition from being partner-dependent communicators to independent communicators.

REFERENCES

Benson, D. F., & Ardilla, A. (1996). *Aphasia: A clinical perspective.* New York, NY: Oxford University Press.
Beukelman, D. R., & Mirenda, P. (2005). *Augmentative and alternative communication: Supporting children and adults with complex communication needs* (3rd ed.). Baltimore, MD: Paul H. Brookes.

Brookshire, R. H. (2003). *An introduction to neurogenic communication disorders* (6th ed.). St. Louis, MO: Mosby-Year Book.

Fitzgerald, E. (1976). *Straight language for the deaf.* Washington, DC: Alexander Graham Bell Association for the Deaf.

Fox, L. E., Sohlberg, M. M., & Fried-Oken, M. (2001). Effects of conversational topic choice on outcomes of augmentative communication intervention for adults with aphasia. *Aphasiology, 15,* 171–200.

Garret, K., & Beukelman, D. (1992). Augmentative communication approaches for persons with severe aphasia. In: K. Yorkston (Ed.), *Augmentative communication in the medical setting* (pp. 245–321). Tucson, AZ: Communication Skill Builders.

Garret, K., & Beukelman, D. (1995). Changes in the interaction patterns of an individual with severe aphasia given three types of partner support. In: M. Lemme (Ed.), *Clinical aphasiology* (Vol. 23, pp. 237–251). Austin, TX: Pro-ed.

Garret, K., & Beukelman, D. (1998). Adults with aphasia. In: D. Beukelman & P. Mirenda (Eds.), *Augmentative communication: Management of children and adults with severe communication disorders* (2nd ed., pp. 465–500). Baltimore, MD: Paul H. Brookes Publishing Company.

Garrett, K. L., & Lasker, J. P. (2005). Adults with severe aphasia. In: D. R. Beukelman & P. Mirenda (Eds.), *Augmentative and alternative communication: Supporting children and adults with complex communication needs* (3rd ed.). Baltimore, MD: Paul H. Brookes.

Goodglass, H., & Kaplan, E. (1983). *Boston diagnostic examination for aphasia.* Philadelphia, PA: Lea & Febiger.

Kagan, A. (1998). Supported conversation for adults with aphasia: Methods and resources for training conversation partners. *Aphasiology, 12,* 816–830.

Kertesz, A. B. (1982). *Western aphasia battery.* New York, NY: Grune & Stratton.

Koul, R., & Corwin, M. (2003). Efficacy of AAC intervention in chronic severe aphasia. In: R. W. Schlosser, H. H. Arvidson & L. L. Lloyd (Eds.), *The efficacy of augmentative and alternative communication: Toward evidence-based practice* (pp. 449–470). San Diego, CA: Academic Press.

Koul, R., Corwin, M., & Hayes, S. (2005). Production of graphic symbol sentences by individuals with aphasia: Efficacy of a computer-based augmentative and communication intervention. *Brain and Language, 92,* 58–77.

Koul, R., Corwin, M., Nigam, R., & Oetzel, S. (2008). Training individuals with severe Broca's aphasia to produce sentences using graphic symbols: Implications for AAC intervention. *Journal of Assistive Technologies, 2,* 23–34.

Koul, R., & Harding, R. (1998). Identification and production of graphic symbols by individuals with aphasia: Efficacy of a software application. *Augmentative and Alternative Communication, 14,* 11–24.

Koul, R., Petroi, D., & Schlosser, R. (2010). Systematic review of speech generating devices for aphasia. In: S. Stern & J. W. Mullennix (Eds.), *Computer synthesized speech technologies: Tools for aiding impairment* (pp. 148–160). Hershey, PA: IGI Global.

Lasker, J. P., & Bedrosian, J. L. (2001). Promoting acceptance of augmentative and alternative communication by adults with acquired communication disorders. *Augmentative and Alternative Communication, 17,* 149–153.

Lasker, J., Garret, K., & Fox, L. (2007). Severe aphasia. In: K. Beukelman & K. Yorkston (Eds.), *Augmentative communication strategies for adults and acute or chronic medical conditions* (pp. 163–206). Baltimore, MD: Paul H. Brookes.

Lasker, J., Hux, K., Garret, K., Moncrief, E., & Eischied, T. (1997). Variations on the written choice communication strategy for individuals with severe aphasia. *Augmentative and Alternative Communication, 13*, 108–116.

Lloyd, L. L., Fuller, D. R., & Arvidson, H. H. (1997). *Augmentative and alternative communication: A handbook of principles and practices.* Needham Heights, MA: Allyn & Bacon.

McKelvey, M. L., Dietz, A. R., Hux, K., Weissling, K., & Beukelman, D. R. (2007). Performance of a person with chronic aphasia using personal and contextual pictures in a visual scene display prototype. *Journal of Medical Speech-Language Pathology, 15*, 305–317.

Mountcastle, V. B. (1978). An organizing principle for cerebral function: The unit module and the distributed system. In: G. M. Edelman & V. B. Mountcastle (Eds.), *The mindful brain: Cortical organization and the group – selective theory of higher brain function* (pp. 7–50). Cambridge, MA: MIT Press.

Porch, B. E. (1981). *Porch index of communicative ability* (3rd ed.). Palo Alto, CA: Consulting Psychologists Press.

Rostron, A., Ward, S., & Plant, R. (1996). Computerised augmentative communication devices for people with dysphasia: Design and evaluation. *European Journal of Disorders of Communication, 31*, 11–30.

Todman, J., & Alm, N. (2003). Modelling conversational pragmatics in communications aids. *Journal of Pragmatics, 35*, 523–538.

Wasson, C. A., Arvidson, H. H., & Lloyd, L. (1997). Low technology. In: L. L. Lloyd, D. R. Fuller & H. H. Arvidson (Eds.), *Augmentative and alternative communication: A handbook of principles and practices* (pp. 127–136). Needham Heights, MA: Allyn and Bacon.

Ward-Lonergan, J. M., & Nicholas, M. (1995). Drawing to communicate: A case report of an adult with global aphasia. *European Journal of Disorders of Communication, 30*, 475–491.

CHAPTER 4

EFFICACY OF TECHNOLOGICALLY BASED AAC INTERVENTION APPROACHES

Rajinder Koul

INTRODUCTION

With the advent of evidence-based practice in health care defined as "finding, appraising, and using contemporaneous research findings as the basis for clinical decisions" (Rosenberg & Donald, 1995, p. 1122), it has become critical to evaluate the evidence about the efficacy of technologically based augmentative and alternative communication (AAC) intervention in persons with aphasia. Schlosser and Raghavendra (2004) defined evidence-based practice in AAC as "the integration of best and current research evidence with clinical/educational expertise and relevant stakeholders perspectives, in order to facilitate decisions about assessment and intervention that are deemed effective and efficient for a given direct stakeholder" (p. 3). The primary purpose of this chapter is to systematically review AAC intervention studies that involved technology as one of the treatment components for individuals with aphasia. The objectives of this review are (1) to describe characteristics of the included studies (e.g., participants, time post-onset, severity of aphasia, and target behaviors), (2) to evaluate intervention outcomes, (3) to appraise the methodological quality of intervention studies, (4) summarize the results of studies that were

Augmentative and Alternative Communication for Adults with Aphasia
Augmentative and Alternative Communications Perspectives, Volume 3, 65–78
Copyright © 2011 by Emerald Group Publishing Limited
All rights of reproduction in any form reserved
ISSN: 2047-0991/doi:10.1108/S2047-0991(2011)0000003010

not included in the systematic review because of methodological concerns, and (5) to identify gaps in the available data to highlight areas for future research.

METHODS

A systematic review methodology was utilized to limit bias in locating, appraising, and synthesizing all relevant AAC intervention studies. This involved a comprehensive search for treatment studies using various databases (e.g., Cumulative Index for Allied Health Literature (CINAHL), PubMed, and Educational Resources in Education Clearinghouse (ERIC)), hand searches of selected journals, as well as ancestry searches. Database searches, including bibliographic database searches (e.g., Academy of Neurologic Communication Disorders and Sciences (ANCDS)), involved locating articles using specific search terms (e.g., AAC and aphasia), and/or searching for articles specifically related to aphasia intervention and/or AAC intervention. Relevant journals (e.g., *AAC* and *Aphasiology*) were also selectively hand searched for potentially relevant articles. Ancestry searches involved examining reference lists of previously published studies related to AAC intervention and aphasia. Each of the search methods utilized involved reviewing titles, abstracts, and/or full-text articles to determine the relevancy of each study. The author and a graduate student in communication sciences and disorders independently decided on study inclusion. Once relevant studies were found, inclusion criteria were applied to determine which articles met the criteria and could be further analyzed. Any disagreements were resolved through a consensus process.

INCLUSION CRITERIA

To be included in this review, the article had to describe a research study that included the provision of an AAC intervention using technology with at least one participant with a diagnosis of aphasia. Additionally, the dependent variables of the studies related to outcomes in which some type of change in behavior was observed secondary to AAC intervention. These included, but were not limited to the identification and manipulation of graphic symbols, production of words, phrases and/or sentences using graphic symbols, and functional communication using either dedicated speech-generating devices (SGDs) and/or graphic symbols or text-based software programs that turn computers into speech output communication devices. Furthermore, only studies that ruled out internal validity concerns by using appropriate single-subject or group experimental designs were included in the review. Finally, studies that focused only on assessment or description of communicative behavior were excluded.

DATA EXTRACTION

Each identified study was first assessed for inclusion/exclusion. Then, each included study was summarized in terms of the following features: (1) participant characteristics such as age, gender, lesion site, time post-onset, and cause; (2) aphasia severity and type; (3) speech and language skills before the brain injury; (4) length of treatment; (5) density of treatment schedule; (6) target-dependent measures; (7) research design; (8) intervention procedures; and (9) outcomes. Each single-subject experimental design study and group study was also individually appraised for methodological quality using the framework proposed by Schlosser and Raghavendra (2003).

Appraising the methodological quality of each study involved assessing the study on several distinct dimensions (Schlosser & Wendt, 2006). The evaluation criteria for single-subject design studies (SSDs) among other criteria included (1) a demonstration of experimental control within a single participant and across different participants, (2) operationally defined independent and dependent variables allowing for replication, and (3) appropriate interobserver agreement and treatment integrity data. Evaluation criteria for group design studies among other criteria included that (1) threats to internal validity were satisfactorily ruled out, (2) data were analyzed using appropriate statistical techniques so that effect size could be determined, and (3) a control condition and/or a control group were included.

RESULTS

Table 1 summarizes the participant characteristics, dependent measures, and outcomes of the included studies.

Table 1. Summary of Results for Single-Subject and Group Design Studies.

Study Authors	Number of Subjects	Range of Time Post-Onset	Severity/Type of Aphasia	Dependent Variable(s)	Research Design	Results
Koul et al. (2008)	$N = 3$	12–106 months	3 Severe Broca's	1. Producing sentences of varied grammatical complexity using graphic symbols	Multiple baseline across behaviors replicated across subjects	All participants were able to combine symbols to produce two-to three-word constructions with high degree of accuracy
McKelvey et al. (2007)	$N = 1$	96 months	Broca's	Use of Visual Scene Displays during conversation interactions: 1. Disability talk instances 2. Navigation/ organization talk instances 3. Inappropriate question-answer exchanges	Multiple baseline across behaviors	The participant demonstrated improvement to varying levels in all three target behaviors
Koul et al. (2005)	$N = 9$	12–105 months	7 Severe Broca's 2 Global	1. Producing sentences of varying grammatical complexity using graphic symbols	Multiple baseline across behaviors replicated across subjects	All participants with Broca's aphasia and one participant with global were able to identify and combine graphic symbols to produce sentences of varying degrees of syntactical complexity. One participant with global aphasia was not able to produce any sentences correctly

Study	N	Time post-onset	Aphasia type	Task	Design	Results
Nicholas et al. (2005)	N = 5	18–90 months	5 Severe non-fluent	Use of *C-Speak Aphasia* during functional communication tasks: 1. Responding to questions 2. Describing pictures 3. Describing videos 4. Making phone calls 5. Writing	Multiple baseline across behaviors replicated across subjects	The performance of all participants on target behaviors was better in the C-Speak condition than the condition without C-Speak
Van de Sandt-Koenderman et al. (2005)	N = 22 (included subjects with LHD[a], RHD[b], subarachnoid hemorrhage, and traumatic brain injury)	30 months	Not specified – limited verbal expression but fairly good auditory comprehension	1. Number of therapy sessions required for PCAD[c] training 2. Outcome of PCAD training 3. Mean age and time post-onset for successful and unsuccessful subjects	Within subject design	All participants were able to use PCAD after intervention, and 77% of the participants used PCAD in functional settings. Time post-onset had no impact on successful outcomes and older participants tended to be more successful in using PCAD than younger participants
Beck and Fritz (1998)	N = 20 Aphasia group: n = 10 Control group: n = 10	≥6 months	Anterior lesions (high comprehension): n = 5 Posterior lesions (low comprehension): n = 5	1. Recalling abstract vs. concrete icon messages using IntroTalker SGD[d] 2. Recalling one, two, and three icon messages using IntroTalker SGD	Between group design	Across all participants, a significantly fewer number of iconic codes were learned for abstract messages than for concrete messages. Additionally, participants with Wernicke's aphasia demonstrated greater difficulty in learning codes for abstract messages than participants with Broca's aphasia

Table 1. (*Continued*)

Study Authors	Number of Subjects	Range of Time Post-Onset	Severity/Type of Aphasia	Dependent Variable(s)	Research Design	Results
Koul and Harding (1998)	$N = 5$	8–60 months	3 Severe Aphasia 2 Global	1. Identification of single symbols 2. Identification of two-symbol combinations	Multiple baseline design across behaviors replicated across subjects	Participants were able to identify and combine symbols to produce short phrases with varying degrees of accuracy. Higher percent correct identification scores were obtained for noun symbols in contrast to symbols from other grammatical classes

[a]LHD, Left hemisphere damage.
[b]RHD, Right hemisphere damage.
[c]PCAD, Portable communication assistant for people with dysphasia.
[d]SGD, Speech-generating device.

Participant Characteristics

Five SSD studies involving a total of 23 participants and two group design studies involving 42 participants with aphasia met the inclusion criteria. The number of participants in SSD studies ranged from 1 to 9, with the mean age of 63.73 years and age range from 27 to 86 years. Forty-eight percent ($n = 11$) of the total participants were male and 52% ($n = 12$) were female. Mean months time post-onset of aphasia was 52.65 months (range = 8–106 months) for 22 of the 23 participants. Data on time post-onset was not available for one of the participants. All participants in SSD studies demonstrated either global aphasia or severe Broca's aphasia.

The data provided on participant characteristics varied across group design studies. However, most of the participants had severe aphasia with limited functional speech. Mean time post-onset of aphasia ranged from equal to or greater than 6–30 months.

Dependent Measures

The targeted skills that were measured in SSD studies included identification of graphic symbols, phrase and sentence production using graphic symbols, and learning to use SGDs in structured as well as functional treatment contexts. The dependent variables measured in the two group design studies that met the inclusion criteria were recall of abstract and concrete icons, recall of one, two, and three icon messages (Beck & Fritz, 1998), and number of therapy sessions required for SGD training, as well as the effect of mean age and time post-onset on training outcome (Van de Sandt-Koenderman, Wiegers, & Hardy, 2005).

Design

All five SSD studies used a multiple baseline design. One group design study used a between group design and the other a within subject design.

Outcomes

Study outcomes were classified as positive, negative, or mixed based on the criteria proposed by Rispoli, Machalicek, and Lang (2010). Studies in which the data indicated that the dependent measures improved for all participants were classified as studies with positive outcomes. Negative outcomes referred to studies in which the data indicated that the dependent measures did not change as a result of AAC intervention. Studies in which at least half of the participants demonstrated improvement in all of the dependent measures targeted were classified as studies with mixed outcomes.

SSD studies with positive outcomes included Koul and Harding (1998), Koul, Corwin, Nigam, and Oetzel (2008), and McKelvey, Dietz, Hux, Weissling, and Beukelman (2007). Koul and Harding used a multiple baseline design across behaviors replicated across three participants with severe aphasia and two with global aphasia to determine whether individuals with aphasia can identify single and multiple symbols from different grammatical categories using a graphic symbol software program that turns a computer into an SGD. Their results indicated that all the participants acquired the basic skills necessary to identify and manipulate the symbols presented across several screens. Noun symbols were identified with a higher degree of accuracy across participants than symbols from other grammatical classes.

Koul et al. (2008) investigated the ability of three individuals with severe Broca's aphasia to produce graphic symbol sentences of varying levels of syntactical complexity using an SGD. A single-subject multiple-baseline design across behaviors replicated across three participants was used to assess the effect of AAC intervention on the production of sentences using graphic symbols. Results indicated that individuals with severe Broca's aphasia were able to combine graphic symbols to produce sentences of varying levels of syntactical complexity. McKelvey et al. (2007), using a multiple baseline design across behaviors, investigated the use of visual scene displays by one person with Broca's aphasia. The dependent variables measured were (1) the number of instances in which the participant talked about his disability, (2) the number of instances in which the participant discussed the navigation of the system, and (3) the number of instances in which the participant asked a question and then answered it himself. The results indicated that the participant demonstrated improvement toward desired levels in all three target behaviors. Nicholas, Sinotte, and Helms-Estabrooks (2005) investigated the use of the C-Speak Aphasia program using a multiple baseline design across subjects replicated across behaviors in five individuals with severe non-fluent aphasia. The target behaviors included several measures: responding to questions, communicating on the telephone, describing pictures and videos, and writing. Results indicated that overall performance across all tasks and participants was superior when they used the C-Speak Aphasia program in contrast to their performance when they were not using the C-Speak program.

The Koul, Corwin, and Hayes (2005) study reported mixed outcomes. The study employed a single-subject multiple baseline design across behaviors replicated across subjects to examine the ability of seven individuals with severe Broca's aphasia and two individuals with global aphasia to produce graphic symbol sentences of varying syntactical complexity using a software program that turns a computer into an SGD. The sentences ranged in complexity from simple two-word phrases to those with morphological inflections, transformations, and relative clauses. Overall, results indicated that all seven individuals with severe Broca's aphasia and one person with global aphasia were able to access, manipulate, and combine graphic symbols to produce phrases and sentences of varying degrees of grammatical complexity. However, one person with global aphasia was not able to produce any sentences correctly. Furthermore, the performance of the participants on the generalization probes was poorer than their performance on the intervention probes. Out of the nine participants with aphasia, only four were able to produce the generalization sentences. Thus, the poor performance on the generalization task by five of the nine participants and the performance of one participant with global aphasia who was unable to produce any sentences in response to intervention probes resulted in classification of this study under mixed outcomes. There were no included SSD studies that had negative outcomes.

Both of the group design studies that met the inclusion criteria had positive outcomes (Beck & Fritz, 1998; Van de Sandt-Koenderman et al., 2005). Beck and Fritz, using a between group design, investigated the ability of five individuals with Broca's aphasia and five individuals with Wernicke's aphasia to recall abstract and concrete iconic messages using an SGD. Results indicated that across all participants, a significantly fewer number of iconic codes were learned for abstract messages than for concrete messages. Furthermore, individuals with Wernicke's aphasia had significantly greater difficulty in learning iconic codes for abstract messages than persons with Broca's aphasia. Van de Sandt-Koenderman et al. (2005) investigated the use of a Portable Communication Assistant for people with Dysphasia (PCAD) by 22 individuals with limited verbal expression but fairly good auditory comprehension. Dependent measures included the number of therapy sessions required for PCAD training and the outcome of the training. Also, the relationship between a positive PCAD outcome and mean age and time post-onset was determined using post hoc analysis. Results indicated that all participants were able to use the PCAD after intervention, and 77% of the participants used PCAD in functional communicative situations. Time post-onset brain injury had no impact on successful outcome.

There were no studies that met the inclusion criteria that were classified as having mixed or negative outcomes.

Appraisal of Evidence

The methodological quality of each study was appraised using the framework proposed by Schlosser and Raghavendra (2003). They described four basic types of research evidence: inconclusive evidence, suggestive evidence, preponderant evidence, and conclusive evidence. Inconclusive evidence suggests that one must be skeptical about the results of the study and its clinical/educational implications because of the serious threats to internal validity. Suggestive evidence indicates that the study may have either minor design flaws or insufficient reliability data. Preponderant evidence suggests that the study may have a strong design with insufficient reliability data or a minor design flaw with adequate reliability data. Conclusive evidence suggests that the study has both a strong design and adequate reliability data. Thus, the methodological quality of Koul et al. (2005) was coded as conclusive as it provided both acceptable interobserver agreement and treatment integrity data. This study also used a controlled experimental design with replication across multiple subjects. However, the Nicholas et al. (2005) study was coded as inconclusive because the study suffered from several internal validity concerns, and data on interobserver agreement or treatment integrity was not provided. Furthermore, the Koul and Harding (1998), Koul et al. (2008), and McKelvey et al. (2007) studies were coded as providing preponderant evidence because these studies used a controlled experimental design and provided acceptable interobserver agreement data. However, these three studies lacked treatment integrity data.

Both of the group design studies that met the inclusion criteria suffered from serious methodological limitations. The Van de Sandt-Koenderman et al. (2005) study did not include a control group or a control condition resulting in serious concerns related to internal validity. In contrast, Beck and Fritz (1998) was relatively stronger because it included a control group. However, the small number of subjects in their study reduces the power of their results and conclusions.

SUMMARY OF STUDIES NOT INCLUDED IN THE SYSTEMATIC REVIEW

The following published studies were not included in the preceding systematic review because they did not meet the inclusion criteria. However, it is important to report these studies here in spite of methodological concerns because of their relevance to clinical practice in the area of AAC and aphasia.

Rostron, Ward, and Plant (1996) described the use of a graphic symbol software program (*EasySpeaker for Windows*) by an individual with severe apraxia and aphasia. The results of this case study indicated that the participant was both able to access the software program and identify and combine symbols that were arranged in a hierarchical fashion across several screens. However, the participant did not use the symbol software program in functional communicative situations.

Van de Sandt-Koenderman, Wiegers, Wielaert, Duivenvoorden, and Ribbers (2007) investigated the use of *TouchSpeak software* by individuals with global and Broca's aphasia using a pretest-posttest single-group design study. The *TouchSpeak software* was installed on a handheld device with options to use both text and symbols. This software has several modules, and each module can be individualized to meet the specific needs of the user. Results indicated that almost half of the persons with aphasia were able to use the software and access the programmed vocabulary. Furthermore, communicative abilities, through the use of a formal test of communicative skills, were also evaluated. A 10% increase in communicative abilities was reported.

Seale, Garrett, and Figley (2007) did a comparative evaluation of two types of vocabulary displays (VSD and traditional grid) on conversational interactions between three people with severe aphasia and their conversational partners. The dependent variables included participants with aphasia telling a personal story using the symbols displayed on their SGD in either VSD or traditional grid format and recall of the same story 3–7 days after the initial storytelling session. Results indicated superior recall of the story when the symbols depicting story elements were displayed in a VSD format in contrast to traditional grid format.

Steele, Aftonomos, and Koul (2010) retrospectively analyzed data obtained from 20 individuals with global aphasia who were trained to use a Lingraphica® SGD. Dependent measures were the scores at intake and discharge on the Western Aphasia Battery (WAB) (Kertesz, 1982) and the

Communicative Effectiveness Index (CETI) (Lomas et al., 1989). The CETI is used to measure functional communication of individuals with aphasia as reported by their caregivers. Results indicated that the participants demonstrated significant improvement in scores from intake to discharge in the auditory verbal comprehension and naming subtest of the WAB. However, no statistically significant change was observed in the spontaneous speech and repetition subtests of the WAB. Furthermore, ratings by the communication partners indicated that significant improvement was observed in 14 of the 16 CETI questions. The magnitude of the improvement across CETI questions ranged from 4.8% to 19%.

Johnson, Hough, King, Vos, and Jeffs (2008) trained three individuals with chronic non-fluent aphasia to use an SGD in which the symbols were hierarchically organized across semantic categories. The vocabulary programmed in SGDs was customized for each participant to meet her/his interests and needs. Dependent measures that were tested before the training and following completion of the training included scores on the following tests or scales: WAB (Kertesz, 1982), Functional Assessment of Communication Skills (FACS) (Frattali, Thompson, Holland, Wohl, & Ferketic, 1995), Quality of Communication Life Scale (QCL) (Paul et al., 2003), and CETI (Lomas et al., 1989). Results indicated significant improvement in the overall aphasia quotient on the WAB for only one of the three participants. However, all three participants demonstrated improvement in the auditory comprehension subtest of the WAB. Additionally, all three participants showed some improvement on FACS and CETI scores indicating that SGD training may have had a positive impact on functional communication. The scores on the QCL from pretest to posttest did not change for two of the three participants.

In summary, the review of these studies indicates that there is a strong potential that technology, if used effectively, can enhance the communicative outcomes for persons with aphasia.

CONCLUSIONS

This chapter presented a systematic review of studies that investigated the efficacy of technologically based AAC intervention in persons with chronic severe Broca's and global aphasia. Overall, results indicate that persons with chronic severe Broca's and global aphasia are able to use dedicated SGDs or graphic symbol software programs that turn computers into SGDs to identify, select, and combine symbols to produce sentences and simple phrases in a variety of settings. Furthermore, persons with aphasia seem to demonstrate superior performance on tasks that involve graphic symbols in contrast to similar tasks that involve production of spoken language. However, the variability of results within and across studies is indicative of the critical need for additional research using well-controlled experimental designs. It is important that future research focus on collecting outcome data on AAC interventions using designs that rule out concerns related to internal and external validity. To adequately support persons with aphasia in maximizing their full inclusion, social integration, employment, and independent living, it is critical to know which interventions work and which interventions work better than others. Unfortunately, the serious paucity of controlled data precludes us from making predictions about the magnitude of treatment effects as a result of technologically based AAC intervention in persons with aphasia.

REFERENCES

Beck, A. R., & Fritz, H. (1998). Can people who have aphasia learn iconic codes? *Augmentative and Alternative Communication, 14*, 184–196.

Frattali, C. M., Thompson, C. K., Holland, A. L., Wohl, C. B., & Ferketic, M. M. (1995). *American Speech-Language-Hearing Association Functional Assessment of Communication Skills for adults (ASHA FACS)*. Rockville, MD: American Speech-Language-Hearing Association.

Johnson, R. K., Hough, M. S., King, K. A., Vos, P., & Jeffs, T. (2008). Functional communication in individuals with chronic severe aphasia using augmentative communication. *Augmentative and Alternative Communication, 24*, 269–280.

Kertesz, A. B. (1982). *Western aphasia battery*. New York, NY: Grune & Stratton.

Koul, R., Corwin, M., & Hayes, S. (2005). Production of graphic symbol sentences by individuals with aphasia: Efficacy of a computer-based augmentative and communication intervention. *Brain and Language, 92*, 58–77.

Koul, R., Corwin, M., Nigam, R., & Oetzel, S. (2008). Training individuals with severe Broca's aphasia to produce sentences using graphic symbols: Implications for AAC intervention. *Journal of Assistive Technologies, 2*, 23–34.

Koul, R., & Harding, R. (1998). Identification and production of graphic symbols by individuals with aphasia: Efficacy of a software application. *Augmentative and Alternative Communication, 14*, 11–24.

Lomas, J., Pickard, L., Bester, S., Elbard, H., Finlayson, A., & Zoghaib, C. (1989). The Communicative Effectiveness Index: Development and psychometric evaluation of a functional communication measure for adult aphasia. *Journal of Speech and Hearing Disorders, 54*, 113–124.

McKelvey, M. L., Dietz, A. R., Hux, K., Weissling, K., & Beukelman, D. R. (2007). Performance of a person with chronic aphasia using personal and contextual pictures in a visual scene display prototype. *Journal of Medical Speech-Language Pathology, 15*, 305–317.

Nicholas, M., Sinotte, M. P., & Helms-Estabrooks, N. (2005). Using a computer to communicate: Effect of executive function impairments in people with severe aphasia. *Aphasiology*, *19*, 1052–1065.

Paul, D. R., Frattali, C. M., Holland, A. L., Thompson, C. K., Caperton, C. J., & Slater, S. C. (2003). *ASHA Quality of Communication Life Scale (QCL)*. Rockville, MD: American Speech-Language-Hearing Association.

Rispoli, M., Machalicek, W., & Lang, R. (2010). Subject review: Communication interventions for individuals with acquired brain injury. *Developmental Neurorehabilitation*, *13*, 141–151.

Rosenberg, W., & Donald, A. (1995). Evidence based medicine: An approach to clinical problem-solving. *British Medical Journal*, *310*, 1122–1126.

Rostron, A., Ward, S., & Plant, R. (1996). Computerized augmentative communication devices for people with dysphasia: Design and evaluation. *European Journal of Disorders of Communication*, *31*, 11–30.

Schlosser, R. W., & Raghavendra, P. (2003). Toward evidence-based practice in AAC. In: R. W. Schlosser, H. H. Arvidson & L. L. Lloyd (Eds.), *The efficacy of augmentative and alternative communication: Toward evidence-based practice* (pp. 259–297). San Diego, CA: Academic Press.

Schlosser, R. W., & Raghavendra, P. (2004). Evidence-based practice in augmentative and alternative communication. *Augmentative and Alternative Communication*, *20*, 1–21.

Schlosser, R. W., & Wendt, O. (2006). *The effects of AAC intervention on speech production in autism: A coding manual and form*. Unpublished manuscript. Northeastern University, Boston, MA.

Seale, J. M., Garrett, K. L., & Figley, L. (2007). Quantitative differences in aphasia interactions with visual scenes AAC displays. Poster presented at the 2007 Clinical AAC Research Conference, Lexington, KY.

Steele, R., Aftonomos, & Koul. (2010). Outcome improvements in persons with chronic global aphasia following the use of a speech-generating device. *Acta Neuropsychologica*, *8*, 342–350.

Van de Sandt-Koenderman, M., Wiegers, J., & Hardy, P. (2005). A computerized communication aid for people with aphasia. *Disability and Rehabilitation*, *27*, 529–533.

Van de Sandt-Koenderman, W. M., Wiegers, J., Wielaert, S. M., Duivenvoorden, H. J., & Ribbers, G. M. (2007). A computerised communication aid in severe aphasia: An exploratory study. *Disability and Rehabilitation*, *29*, 1701–1709.

CHAPTER 5

EFFICACY OF NO-TECHNOLOGY-BASED AAC INTERVENTION APPROACHES

Melinda Corwin

INTRODUCTION

Augmentative and alternative communication (AAC) is often discussed in terms of the amount and type of technology involved. Garrett and Lasker (2005) promoted assessing a person with aphasia for his or her potential to employ various AAC tools by asking which of the following means of communication the person typically uses: unaided strategies, partner-dependent (also known as partner-assisted) strategies, use of external stored information, and/or use of self-formulated/self-generated messages. When these forms of communication are used without electronic technology that results in synthetic or digitized speech output, they are termed *no-technology* AAC options. These no-technology forms of AAC are described in the following paragraphs.

STRATEGY TYPES

Unaided Strategies

Unaided AAC strategies include those which involve only the person's own body (without external aids), such as hand gestures, body position, prosody,

Augmentative and Alternative Communication for Adults with Aphasia
Augmentative and Alternative Communications Perspectives, Volume 3, 79–92
Copyright © 2011 by Emerald Group Publishing Limited
All rights of reproduction in any form reserved
ISSN: 2047-0991/doi:10.1108/S2047-0991(2011)0000003011

facial expression, pointing, pantomiming, stereotypic utterances, and head nodding/shaking. When used in a discernible manner, these strategies allow the person with aphasia to successfully convey messages, especially responses to simple questions. These strategies are somewhat dependent on the communication partner's ability to correctly interpret the intended meaning of the person with aphasia. Communication partners who have a close relationship and/or are more familiar with the person who has aphasia may experience more success in correctly interpreting alternative, unaided forms of communication than communication partners who are less close and/or less familiar. Examples of the use of unaided AAC strategies by a person with aphasia are provided below.

Communication partner: "What do you want?"

Person with aphasia: [Strokes cheek with left hand.]

Communication partner: "A washcloth?"

Person with aphasia: [Shakes head no.]

Communication partner: "Does your face itch?"

Person with aphasia: [Shakes head no; slowly strokes bent index finger along one cheek and then the other.]

Communication partner: "Oh, your razor?"

Person with aphasia: [Nods affirmatively; smiles.]

Partner-Dependent/Partner-Assisted Strategies

Partner-dependent or partner-assisted strategies include the communication partner's use of augmented input and/or written-choice communication (Garrett & Beukelman, 1995, 1998; Garrett & Lasker, 2005). Augmented input serves to enhance comprehension of the topic/message by the person with aphasia. The communication partner uses all available visual modalities to accompany a spoken message, including written words, sketches, gestures, and pointing to or manipulating actual objects (e.g., calendars and clocks). The communication partner selects simple and familiar contexts, identifies communication topics of interest, and initiates interaction (Garrett & Beukelman, 1995, 1998). In written-choice communication, the partner provides the person with aphasia with written word choices to point to in response to questions (Lasker, 2001). Because this method involves cued rather than free recall, it may facilitate responses from persons with chronic severe and/or global aphasia. The written-choice communication strategy is only helpful if the person with aphasia possesses sufficient residual reading and auditory processing abilities. Persons with global aphasia demonstrate impairments in all language modalities and thus may not benefit from this strategy. Another limitation is that the communication partner must know the target response in order to provide the correct stimulus among the written choices. Thus, if a discussion ensues between the person with aphasia and a communication partner and the partner is unable to write viable or correct choices, a breakdown in communication may occur.

Another partner-dependent approach known as *supported conversation for adults with aphasia* (SCA™) involves training/teaching communication partners important skills so that they can in turn reveal the communicative competence of the person with aphasia (Kagan, 1995; Kagan, Black, Duchan, Simmons-Mackie, & Square, 2001; Kagan et al., 2004). Another way to describe this approach is as follows: The communication partner provides a *communication ramp* for the person with aphasia (analogous to a wheelchair ramp for a person with a physical disability) so that the person with aphasia can successfully maneuver and participate in a conversation (Kagan & Gailey, 1993).

An example of partner-dependent/partner-assisted interactions involving augmented input and written-choice strategies is provided below:

Communication partner: "I'm [points to self] 39 years old [simulta-neously writes '39' on a piece of paper]. How old were you [points to person with aphasia] when you had your stroke [simultaneously points to head/brain area]? [Writes in large block letters while simultaneously saying

45
46
47
48
NONE OF THE ABOVE]?"

Person with aphasia: [Points to 47.]

Communication partner: "Oh, OK. Where were you living at the time [points to a map of the United States while raising eyebrows]?"

Person with Aphasia: [Points to the western portion of the U.S. map.]

Communication Partner: "Oh, was it one of these [raises eyebrows and writes in large block letters while simultaneously saying

CALIFORNIA
WASHINGTON
NEVADA
ARIZONA]?"

Person with Aphasia: "Yes, there." [Points to CALIFORNIA.]

Communication Partner: "Oh, so you [points to person with aphasia] were working [simultaneously writes WORK] in California [points to state of California on the map] at the time [raises eyebrows]?"

Person with Aphasia: [Nods affirmatively.]

Communication Partner: "Well, when did you [points to person with aphasia] move here to Texas [points to state of Texas on the map] [raises eyebrows and writes in large block letters while simultaneously saying

2008
2009
2010
NONE OF THE ABOVE]?"

Person with Aphasia: "Uh ... nine." [Points to 2009]

Communication Partner: "2009? So you've been here for a few years now [gestures counting on fingers]. Do you [points to person with aphasia] live alone [sketches a house with a stick figure person in it and writes '2011' above the sketch]?"

Person with Aphasia: [Nods affirmatively.]

Communication Partner: "Have you always lived alone [points to house/person sketch]? I thought initially you lived with someone – a relative, perhaps [sketches a different house with three stick figures in it and writes '2009' above the sketch]?"

Person with Aphasia: [Nods affirmatively.] "Yes!" [Points to stick figures in house sketch] "Oh, I can't." (Sighs.)

Communication Partner: "Hmmm ... was it [points to stick figures in house sketch] your ... [writes in large block letters while simultaneously saying
MOTHER

FATHER
AUNT
SISTER
NONE OF THE ABOVE]?"

Person with Aphasia: [Points to AUNT and smiles.]

Communication Partner: "Oh, I thought I remembered [points to own head] it was a relative [points to the word AUNT]. Are you glad to be living alone now [sketches a happy face beside the 2011 house]?"

Person with Aphasia: [Nods affirmatively and smiles.]

External-Stored Information

The external-stored information strategy involves a person using an alternative mode of communication that has an external source for information. The external source may involve high technology, such as an electronic device with a voice-output system (as discussed in other chapters), or no technology, such as an album with personal photographs and/or remnants, a communication board or book with established pictures or written words, or an object which can be touched or otherwise manipulated. The person with aphasia is limited by his or her ability to successfully retrieve and convey concepts with the external stored information that is available. When successful, the person with aphasia is an independent communicator. A real-life example using external-stored information but no technology is provided below:

Person with aphasia: "I ... uh ... here." [Opens Communication Note-book and points to a photograph with a date printed on it.]

Communication partner: "I see you were with someone this weekend. Is that your son?"

Person with aphasia: "Yes!"

Communication partner: "He's handsome. Where does he live?"

Person with aphasia: "Uh ... uh ... " [Flips to another page in Communication Notebook titled *Family Members*. Points to a name, address, and telephone number.]

Communication partner: "Ah, he lives in Arkansas."

Person with aphasia: [Flips to another page with a family photo and caption underneath.]

Communication partner: "Is that his family?"

Person with aphasia: [Nods affirmatively and smiles.]

Communication partner: "Your grandsons ... [reads aloud photo caption] Jarred and Jackson. They're cute."

Person with aphasia: [Smiles proudly and points to photo.] "My ... grandsons!"

Self-Formulated/Self-Generated Messages

The self-formulated or self-generated strategy involves the person with aphasia being a more independent communicator by generating topics or responses, using drawing and/or writing as a substitute or augmentation for spoken language. When successful, this strategy affords communicative independence and success to its user; however, sometimes gestures and drawings are vague or words are misspelled, such that the communication partner must bear much of the conversational burden to ensure that the message is conveyed. Additionally, persons with chronic severe aphasia often have difficulty independently accessing the concept/idea they are trying to convey; thus, writing may be difficult or even impossible. An example of a successful interaction is provided below.

Communication partner: "What did you do this weekend?"

Person with aphasia: [Shrugs shoulders. Pauses 5 seconds. Using the nondominant hand, writes GABLE on a piece of paper.]

Communication partner: "Did you gamble this weekend?"

Person with aphasia: [Nods affirmatively.] "Yes!"

Communication partner: "Sounds fun. Did you win anything?"

Person with aphasia: [Nods affirmatively; writes 400 on a piece of paper.]

Communication partner: "$400? Wow, I'll send you with some of my money next time if you'll split the winnings with me!"

Person with aphasia: [Laughs, then furrows brow; draws a series of curved lines on the paper.]

Communication partner: "Are we still talking about gambling?"

Person with aphasia: [Shakes head no.]

Communication partner: "Oh. You're changing the subject. Are you talking about seizures?"

Person with aphasia: [Shakes head no and points to the curved lines.]

Communication partner: "Is that a plant?"

Person with aphasia: [Nods affirmatively.]

Communication partner: "Oh. I'll bet you're asking me how that plant you gave me is doing."

Person with aphasia: [Nods affirmatively and smiles.] "Aha!"

Communication partner: "You'll be impressed. I haven't killed it yet."

Person with aphasia: [Laughs.]

EFFICACY RESEARCH

No-technology AAC intervention approaches range from strategies that are based on the communication participation model (e.g., Fox, Sohlberg, & Fried-Oken, 2001; Kagan, 1995; Kagan et al., 2001, 2004) to those in which individuals with chronic Broca's and/or global aphasia are trained to acquire and use graphic symbols such as pictographs, line drawings, and translucent symbol sets and systems without the aid of technology (e.g., Funnell & Allport, 1989; Lasker, Hux, Garrett, Moncrief, & Eischeid, 1997; Ward-Lonergan & Nicholas, 1995).

Robey and Shultz (1998) described a five-phase model for clinical outcome research in aphasia, adapted from the standard health-care model of clinical outcome research. Phase I involves small group experiments, case studies, and single-subject experiments designed to detect effects of a particular treatment for aphasia. Phase II also involves small group experiments, case studies, and single-subject experiments in which the clinical population, parameters, construct, and environment are clearly defined. Additionally, explicit operational definitions and exploratory estimates of efficacy are provided. Phase III involves pre comparison and post comparison groups that are relatively large and parallel. Multiple-center clinical trials are ideal. The research hypotheses are clearly stated and tested under optimal conditions. Phase IV involves large sample parallel group experiments or highly structured and well controlled single-subject experiments with multiple replications. The purpose of Phase IV research is to assess a particular subpopulation or treatment protocol in a typical (rather than ideal) condition. Phase V involves large group, multiple-replication single-subject, and/or meta-analyses to investigate treatment effectiveness in terms of cost, consumer satisfaction, and quality of life.

Schlosser (2003a) studied various conceptualizations of outcomes and efficacy, including the one posited by Robey and Shultz (1998), and elected to use efficacy as an umbrella term which includes effectiveness, efficiency, and effects of intervention. Schlosser (2003b) noted that efficacy of AAC interventions could be studied under ideal, typical, and less-than-typical conditions using well-designed, appropriate single-subjects experimental designs involving multiple baselines or multiple probes. He also stated that two of the most useful designs in AAC research today include the single-subject adapted alternating-treatment design and the parallel-treatments design.

To date, most research involving no-technology AAC and aphasia has been of the Phases I and II, pre-efficacy type based on Robey and Shultz's (1998) classification system. Case study and single-subject designs are common. According to Schlosser (2003a), if well conceptualized and designed, these studies can provide valuable information in terms of the effectiveness, efficiency, and effects of no-technology AAC intervention. Although results cannot be generalized to the entire clinical population of aphasia, they can begin to inform our discipline in terms of potential ideal treatment for persons with aphasia. Examples of research studies from each of the four types of communication strategies (unaided, partner-dependent/partner-assisted, external stored information, and self-formulated/self-generated messages) are provided in the following sections.

REVIEW OF RESEARCH STUDIES

Unaided Strategies

Coelho (1991) used a single-subject multiple baseline across settings design with two participants with moderate to severe expressive aphasia. The individuals were trained to use 12 iconic manual signs to indicate food items. Training occurred in a clinical setting as well as a simulated restaurant setting. Results revealed that both participants used the trained signs in both settings; however, only one participant used the signs appropriately in a natural setting, and neither of the participants increased their use of signs in their daily environments.

Kraat (1990) and Jacobs, Drew, Ogletree, and Pierce (2004) provided a literature review and summary of unaided and aided AAC treatments for persons with severe aphasia over the past 40 years. The authors concluded that some studies supported the use of unaided (as well as aided) AAC strategies; however, most studies only reported gains in a structured treatment setting but not in natural, everyday settings. They advocated future studies that carefully· control for variables that could affect results, such as user knowledge and ease of system use. They also expressed the need for studies that systematically moved treatment from a structured clinical setting to a natural environment. Finally, they stressed the need to determine the social validity of treatments in terms of their goals, methods, and outcomes.

Partner-Dependent/Partner-Assisted Strategies

As previously described in this chapter, Kagan (1995) discussed an approach known as SCA™. This approach involves a communication partnership between the person with aphasia and the partner without aphasia. The conversational partner willingly and actively shares the communication burden and serves as a resource for the person with aphasia. The partner makes appropriate resource materials available to the person with aphasia and creates an *aphasia-friendly* environment that assumes competence on the part of the person with aphasia. Garrett and Lasker (2005) discussed similar communicator strategies as well as partner strategies that can be employed for persons with aphasia. Communication partners can use various types of communication ramps, based on the characteristics, needs, and level of functioning of the person with aphasia. Thus, several of the tenets of SCA™ are applied in approaches that involve AAC, as evidenced by the study descriptions in the following paragraphs.

Garret and Huth (2002) used a single-subject design to evaluate the use of graphic topic setters by two different communication partners and a person with aphasia. Results revealed that the communication partners were more successful in conversations when graphic topic setters were used, especially with topics involving current events.

Lasker et al. (1997) evaluated the relative effectiveness of three different written-choice communication strategies in enhancing efficiency and quality of communication for three individuals with severe chronic aphasia. Results indicated that the performance varied across participants. Specifically, for a participant with severe Wernicke's aphasia, accuracy scores for a standard written-choice communication condition were superior to auditory-only and visual-only conditions. In contrast, for a participant with severe expressive and moderate receptive aphasia and for another participant with Broca's aphasia, accuracy scores on the standard written-choice communication condition did not differ from the scores obtained for auditory-only and visual-only conditions. This study design did not rule out sequence or carryover effects, and further research is indicated; however, written-choice communication could be an effective treatment and may work better with certain types of aphasia.

Kagan et al. (2001) investigated 20 trained versus 20 untrained conversational partner volunteers interacting with persons who had aphasia. They used a single-blind, randomized, pre-/posttest design. The experimental (trained) group used the SCA™ approach. Results revealed that the trained individuals and their conversational partners with aphasia improved as follows: Volunteer partners trained in SCA™ scored higher than their untrained counterparts in terms of acknowledging and revealing competence in their communication partners with aphasia. Adults with aphasia scored higher in terms of interaction (connecting socially) and transaction (transferring information regarding feelings, facts, or opinions) when they attempted to converse with trained partners as compared to untrained partners. As trained volunteer partners' communication strategies improved, so did the communication strategies of individuals with aphasia. The partners' revelation of competence in the persons with aphasia was most strongly and significantly correlated with successful information transfer (transaction) by the person with aphasia. Kagan et al. (2004) also developed two measures, one for providing an index of the conversation partner's skill and one for providing an index of the level of participation by the person with aphasia. Although further studies are certainly needed, caregiver training using SCA™ seems to be a promising form of AAC intervention.

External Stored Information

Several studies have confirmed that individuals with chronic severe aphasia can acquire and use pictographs, line drawings, and symbol systems such as Blissymbols (Bliss, 1965) (e.g., Koul & Lloyd, 1998; Lane & Samples, 1981; Nishikawa, 1980; Ross, 1979; Sawyer-Woods, 1987). Additional studies have attempted to investigate the use of external stored information to promote interactions with others.

Garrett, Beukelman, and Low-Morrow (1989) described the effectiveness of a multimodal communication system (i.e., word dictionary, alphabet card, information pocket, breakdown resolution clues, conversational control strategies, and natural communication) in an individual with Broca's aphasia. Their results indicated that there were more conversational turns, conversational initiations, communication acts, and fewer communication breakdowns in the posttreatment condition.

Fox et al. (2001) investigated the effects of conversational topic choice on outcomes of AAC intervention in three individuals with Broca's aphasia using an alternating-treatment single-subject design. Participants were assigned to two conditions: choice topic and nonchoice topic. Choice topics were topics of high interest for participants, and nonchoice topics were assigned by the investigators. One participant demonstrated greater use of AAC symbols (i.e., personal photographs, color photographs from magazines, and line drawings with word labels) when discussing choice topics. The other two participants did not demonstrate a difference in the use of AAC symbols between conditions. Thus, results were mixed regarding the benefit of using high-interest choice topics to facilitate communication.

Using an alternating-treatment single-subject design, Ho, Weiss, Garrett, and Lloyd (2005) studied two persons with global aphasia in the spontaneous stage of recovery from stroke. These individuals interacted with a speech-language pathologist under three different conditions: no external stored information available, use of pictographic topic symbols in the form of Picture Communication Symbols (PCS) in a communication book, and use of remnants (e.g., maps, photographs, and magazine covers) in a communication book. Results indicated that the persons with global aphasia had more successful interactions when symbols (either PCS or remnants) were used. They initiated more topics, successfully communicated messages more often, and experienced more positive effects when they had access to a communication book compared to when they did not.

Self-Formulated/Self-Generated Messages

Ward-Lonergan and Nicholas (1995) evaluated the ability of one person with global aphasia to communicate effectively through drawing. The treatment was comprised of tasks that ranged from simple copying of pictures to drawing complex pictures from memory. Results indicated that the posttreatment drawings were rated as much more recognizable by a naive judge than pretreatment drawings. The authors reported that the pretreatment drawings were sketchy and lacked details. A case study design was used, and the project did not fully address the self-formulation or self-generation of messages via drawing. Rather, results revealed that the person's drawing abilities could be refined with practice over time. Other case studies (e.g., Beeson & Ramage, 2000) have also discussed the benefits of self-generated drawing for the purposes of initiating and maintaining communication. Thus, drawing should continue to be investigated as a possible form of no-technology AAC that is formulated and generated by the person with aphasia.

SUMMARY

Several studies have been conducted and lend support for the use of no-technology AAC strategies for persons with aphasia, including unaided, partner-dependent/partner-assisted, and external stored information. Fewer successes have been documented for self-formulated/self-generated messages. Perhaps this is because persons with mild aphasia may be able to generate oral messages independently, especially if given ample time; whereas, persons with severe aphasia seem to have difficulty independently formulating/generating messages, despite the provision of no-technology AAC devices. Conversational partners may play a key role in facilitating (as opposed to discouraging) persons with aphasia to formulate and generate messages by allowing ample wait time, assuming competence on the part of the person with aphasia, and providing conversational supports as needed.

Based on overall research findings to date, we have learned that persons with chronic severe aphasia seem to perform better on tasks that involve graphic symbols in comparison to tasks that involve natural language. We have also learned that AAC intervention that involves multimodalities, includes communication partner training, and uses the communication participation model seems to enhance communicative effectiveness and efficiency of persons with aphasia. AAC intervention for persons with aphasia must be socially and ecologically valid as well (further discussion is provided in Chapters 7 and 8). Additional research is needed to better inform our practice, but we are well on the way to understanding what no-technology forms of AAC intervention have to offer persons with aphasia.

REFERENCES

Beeson, P. M., & Ramage, A. E. (2000). Drawing from experience: The development of alternative communication strategies. *Topics in Stroke Rehabilitation, 7,* 10–20.

Bliss, C. K. (1965). *Semantography: Blissymbolics* (2nd ed.). Sydney, Australia: Semantography Publications.

Coelho, C. (1991). Manual sign acquisition and use in two aphasic subjects. *Clinical Aphasiology, 19,* 445–456.

Fox, L. E., Sohlberg, M. M., & Fried-Oken, M. (2001). Effects of conversational topic choice on outcomes of augmentative communication intervention for adults with aphasia. *Aphasiology, 15,* 171–200.

Funnell, E., & Allport, A. (1989). Symbolically speaking: communicating with Blissymbols in aphasia. *Aphasiology, 3,* 279–300.

Garrett, K. L., & Beukelman, D. R. (1995). Changes in the interaction patterns of an individual with severe aphasia given three types of partner support. In: M. Lemme (Ed.), *Clinical aphasiology* (pp. 237–251). Austin, TX: PRO-ED.

Garrett, K. L., & Beukelman, D. R. (1998). Adults with severe aphasia. In: D. R. Beukelman & P. Mirenda (Eds.), *Augmentative and alternative communication: Management of severe communication disorders in children and adults* (2nd ed., pp. 465–499). Baltimore: Paul H. Brookes.

Garrett, K. L., Beukelman, D. R., & Low-Morrow, D. (1989). A comprehensive augmentative communication system for an adult with Broca's aphasia. *Augmentative and Alternative Communication, 5,* 55–61.

Garret, K. L., & Huth, C. (2002). The impact of graphic contextual information and instruction on the conversational behaviours of a person with severe aphasia. *Aphasiology, 16*(4/5/6), 523–536.

Garrett, K. L., & Lasker, J. P. (2005). AAC for adults with severe aphasia. In: D. Beukelman & P. Mirenda (Eds.), *Augmentative and alternative communication for augmentative and alternative communication: Supporting children and adults with complex communication needs* (pp. 467–504). Baltimore, MD: Paul H. Brookes.

Ho, K. M., Weiss, S. J., Garrett, K. L., & Lloyd, L. L. (2005). The effect of remnant and pictographic books on the communicative interaction of individuals with global aphasia. *Augmentative and Alternative Communication, 21*(3), 218–232.

Jacobs, B., Drew, R., Ogletree, B. T., & Pierce, K. (2004). Augmentative and alternative communication (AAC) for adults with severe aphasia: Where we stand and how we can go further. *Disability and Rehabilitation, 26*(21/22), 1231–1240.

Kagan, A. (1995). Revealing the competence of aphasic adults through conversation: A challenge to health professionals. *Topics in Stroke Rehabilitation, 2,* 15–28.

Kagan, A., Black, S., Duchan, J., Simmons-Mackie, N., & Square, P. (2001). Training volunteers as conversational partners using supported conversation for adults with aphasia (SCA™). *Journal of Speech, Language, and Hearing Research, 44,* 624–638.

Kagan, A., & Gailey, G. F. (1993). Functional is not enough. In: A. Holland & M. Forbes (Eds.), *Aphasia treatment: World perspectives* (pp. 199–225). London: Chapman & Hall.

Kagan, A., Winckel, J., Black, S., Duchan, J. F., Simmons-Mackie, N., & Square, P. (2004). A set of observational measures for rating support and participation in conversation between adults with aphasia and their conversation partners. *Topics in Stroke Rehabilitation, 11*(1), 67–83.

Koul, R. K., & Lloyd, L. L. (1998). Comparison of graphic symbol learning in individuals with aphasia and right hemisphere brain damage. *Brain and Language, 62*, 394–421.

Kraat, A. W. (1990). Augmentative and alternative communication: Does it have a future in aphasia rehabilitation? *Aphasiology, 4*, 321–338.

Lane, V. W., & Samples, J. M. (1981). Facilitating communication skills in adult aphasics: Application of Blissymbolics in a group setting. *Journal of Communication Disorders, 14*, 157–167.

Lasker, J. (2001, May). *AAC strategies for adults with aphasia: From picture boards to touch screens.* Paper presented at the Annual Convention of Georgia Speech-Hearing-Language Association, Atlanta, GA.

Lasker, J., Hux, K., Garrett, K. L., Moncrief, E. M., & Eischeid, T. J. (1997). Variations on the written choice communication strategy for individuals with severe aphasia. *Augmentative and Alternative Communication, 13*, 108–116.

Nishikawa, L. K. (1980). *Blissymbolics as an augmentative communication tool for adults with expressive aphasia.* Unpublished Master's thesis, Loma Linda University.

Robey, R. R., & Shultz, M. C. (1998). A model for conducting clinical-outcome research: An adaptation of the standard protocol for use in aphasiology. *Aphasiology, 12*(9), 787–810.

Ross, A. J. (1979). A study of the application of Blissymbols as a means of communication for a young brain damaged adult. *British Journal of Disorders of Communication, 14*, 103–109.

Sawyer-Woods, L. (1987). Symbolic function in a severe non-verbal aphasic. *Aphasiology, 1*, 287–290.

Schlosser, R. W. (2003a). Efficacy and outcomes measurement in augmentative and alternative communication. In: R. Schlosser (Ed.), *The efficacy of augmentative and alternative communication: Toward evidence-based practice* (pp. 13–25). San Diego: Academic Press.

Schlosser, R. W. (2003b). Single-subject experimental designs. In: R. Schlosser (Ed.), *The efficacy of augmentative and alternative communication: Toward evidence-based practice* (pp. 86–144). San Diego: Academic Press.

Ward-Lonergan, J. M., & Nicholas, M. (1995). Drawing to communicate: a case report of an adult with global aphasia. *European Journal of Disorders of Communication, 30*, 475–491.

CHAPTER 6

AAC AND MESSAGE ENHANCEMENT FOR PERSONS WITH APHASIA

Ann R. Beck

INTRODUCTION

Message enhancement for persons with aphasia is a process by which their reduced capacity for communications in writing, speech, or signals can be increased or improved in value, quality, desirability, and attractiveness. The traditional approach to treating communication difficulties of a person with aphasia has been through the use of stimulation-type aphasia interventions in which the person is stimulated with various types of input to facilitate the quality of his or her comprehension and expression of language (Garrett & Lasker, 2005). As Garrett and Lasker pointed out, however, this approach is successful for some people with aphasia, but there are many people with severe aphasia for whom this approach is not successful. People with mild and moderate levels of aphasia may benefit from alternatives that support their natural abilities (Hux, Manasse, Weiss, & Beukelman, 2001). Additional alternative approaches, however, may be needed for people with severe aphasia to regain competency and functionality as communicators.

One alternative approach that can be considered for with persons with aphasia is augmentative and alternative communication (AAC) systems.

Augmentative and Alternative Communication for Adults with Aphasia
Augmentative and Alternative Communications Perspectives, Volume 3, 93–113
Copyright © 2011 by Emerald Group Publishing Limited
All rights of reproduction in any form reserved
ISSN: 2047-0991/doi:10.1108/S2047-0991(2011)0000003012

The use of low-technology AAC strategies (e.g., communication boards, pictures, and written word choices) with persons with aphasia has been documented in case studies for the past 30 years (Beukelman, Fager, Ball, & Dietz, 2007). An increase in the recent use of high-technology AAC options has also been reported (Beukelman, Ball, & Fager, 2008). Thus, AAC approaches that could be considered for people with aphasia range from unaided gestures to simple graphic symbols and to computer-based AAC systems.

Hux et al. (2001) indicated that persons with mild aphasia may require only simple AAC supports, such as word lists, to aid in instances of anomia. People with a more moderate level of aphasia may, however, need to utilize AAC strategies (e.g., gestures, remnant books, letters, or written words) to not only support but also to take the place of natural speech to communicate adequately. Because of their highly reduced ability to communicate naturally, persons with severe aphasia will need a comprehensive AAC system to communicate.

Beukelman and Mirenda (2005) indicated that regardless of the severity of the aphasia or of the type and extent of AAC component(s) used, AAC is primarily about facilitating communication in people so that they are able to interact with others. The key concern for message enhancement then relates to how messages can be presented to and produced by persons with aphasia so that they can communicate functionally with others in their environments. This chapter focuses on issues that should be considered when aiming to increase the social value, quality, and desirability of the messages produced through the use of computer-based AAC systems.

CHARACTERISTICS OF APHASIA AND AAC INTERVENTION

Garrett and Lasker (2005) stated that "by definition, the disorder that is aphasia affects each of the levels of processing that AAC systems demand" (p. 501). While Blackstone (2006) emphasized the fact that there are no cognitive, physical, or situational prerequisites that need to be met before introducing AAC interventions to an adult with an acquired disability, there are "specific skill sets required to operate different types of AAC devices, techniques and strategies" (p. 6). Thus, in considering AAC message enhancement for persons with aphasia, clinicians need to be aware of individual communication strengths and weaknesses and the impact these skill levels and skill sets have on efficient and effective use of various AAC system components.

Darley (1982; as cited by McNeil & Kimelman, 2001, p. 42) defined the condition of aphasia as follows:

> Impairment, as a result of brain damage, of the capacity for interpretation and formulation of language symbols; multimodality loss or reduction in efficiency of the ability to decode and encode conventional meaningful linguistic elements ... disproportionate to impairment of other intellective functions ... and manifested in reduced availability of vocabulary, reduced efficiency in application of syntactic rules, reduced auditory retention span and impaired efficiency in input and output channel selection.

This definition of aphasia clearly indicates that aphasia results in a loss or reduction of a person's ability to utilize meaningful linguistic elements.

According to Beck and Fritz (1998), the type of aphasia a person has can result in different forms of semantic deficits. People with an anterior, nonfluent form of aphasia typically have relatively intact semantic lexicons, whereas individuals with a posterior, fluent form of aphasia often have either a reduction in the information held in their semantic fields or difficulty in accessing meaning of words in their lexicon (Goodglass & Baker, 1976; Grober, Perecman, Kellar, & Brown, 1980). Given that many aided AAC systems make use of graphic symbols in some form, knowledge of the degree to which a person can assign meaning to various types of symbols and of the elements that would facilitate appropriate activation of his or her semantic fields is important.

Another potential area of disability in aphasia is in the application of syntactic rules. If a person has problems with syntactic encoding, as is often found in anterior or nonfluent form of aphasia, he or she may have problems sequencing symbols in grammatically complete and correct forms (Garrett & Lasker, 2005). On the basis of a review of the literature, Kraat (1990) concluded that it is challenging for clinicians to help people with severe aphasia increase their use of signs and symbols from single-word outputs to more grammatically complete productions. Thus, determining the extent of disability in the syntactical abilities of a person with aphasia and how that disability influences the ability to comprehend and produce various augmented messages must be considered when planning AAC interventions.

Persons with aphasia may also demonstrate deficits in processing speed, attention, memory, and problem solving that cannot be completely attributable to their language impairments (Garrett & Lasker, 2005).

Furthermore, the communicative behaviors of persons with aphasia are known to be highly variable (McNeil, 1983). McNeil suggested a model of attention that could help to explain some of the variability found in language behaviors of persons with aphasia. The model posited suggests that there is a single pool of attention, or perhaps more than one independent pool of attention, "which is shared by all or several sensory, integrative, and motor operations, across all or several modalities" (p. 14). The attention that can be allotted to one task or set of tasks at a time is limited and variable. According to Murray, Holland, and Beeson (1997), task demands, or the processing resources needed, determine the amount of attention allocated to any one cognitive task at a specific time. If a person has insufficient resources, or if his or her resources have been allocated to a different task, the attention needed for a task will not be available. Persons with aphasia have been documented as having greater difficulty allocating their attention than individuals without brain damage. Clinicians must consider how these attentional deficits may affect the language skills of their clients and their ability to utilize AAC systems (McNeil, 1983; Murray et al., 1997).

A strength, however, for many persons, even those with severe aphasia, is in the area of visuospatial abilities (Dietz, McKelvey, & Beukelman, 2006; McKelvey, Hux, Dietz, & Beukelman, 2010). While the ability to comprehend written and pantomimed materials is often compromised by aphasia, the ability of persons with aphasia to comprehend and analyze graphic material has been found to be similar to that of persons without aphasia (Koul & Lloyd, 1998; Thorburn, Newhoff, & Rubin, 1995). This preserved ability may be due to the fact that the right hemisphere, the cerebral hemisphere that is typically not impaired in cases of aphasia, is heavily involved in acquiring, retaining, and remembering iconic drawings (Koul & Corwin, 2003). Koul and Corwin pointed out that when a person conveys a message using a graphic rather than a verbal modality, the need for complex morphosyntactic, phonetic, or articulatory processing is not necessary. Therefore, for a person with aphasia, the acquisition and use of graphic symbols (e.g., line drawing, Blissymbolics, and pictographs) for communication may be relatively easier than the use of natural spoken language. As Jacobs, Drew, Ogletree, and Pierce (2004) suggested, there is "an intuitive fit between AAC and persons with severe aphasia" (p. 1238).

Additionally, a consistent finding has been that persons with aphasia can learn the basic skills needed to interface successfully with a computer and symbol software (e.g., Aftonomos, Steele, Appelbaum, & Harris, 2001; Koul & Harding, 1998; McCall, Shelton, Weinrich, & Cox, 2000;

Weinrich, McCall, Weber, Thomas, & Thornburg, 1995). Thus, the use of aided AAC systems, including speech output communication devices, appears to hold promise as a significant communication option for persons with aphasia.

COMPUTER-BASED AAC SYSTEMS AND THEIR USE IN APHASIA INTERVENTION

One of the limitations of aided AAC systems is the speed with which messages can be produced. Typical communicators speak at a rate of 150–250 words per minute, whereas persons who communicate with aided AAC symbols average a rate of 15 words per minute or less (Beukelman & Mirenda, 2005). Beukelman and Mirenda explained that this difference in communication rate results from the fact that persons who use aided AAC strategies need to compose their messages one item at a time from their communication displays. Encoding messages with fewer signals than would be needed by a letter-by-letter or word-by-word formulation of the message is one approach to enhancing the communication rate of a person who uses AAC. Such message-encoding strategies increase the rate of augmented communication by decreasing the number of keystrokes or selections needed to produce the message.

Beukelman and Mirenda (2005) list several different message-encoding strategies. Two of these are *salient-letter encoding* and *letter-category encoding*. In salient-letter encoding, the first letter of each key word is used to encode the message. For example, "Let the dog out." might be encoded as LDO. In letter-category encoding, the first letter of the code stands for the category to which the message belongs, and the remaining letters refer to the specific message within the category. For example, using letter-category encoding, the message "Let the dog out." could be encoded as RDO; R for request and DO for dog out. Beck and Fritz (1998) pointed out that both of these strategies require functional literacy skills and that because persons with aphasia often have impaired literacy skills, such strategies may be difficult to use.

Another message-encoding strategy that does not require functional literacy skills is *iconic encoding*, or the combining of pictures to code a message. Minspeak™ is one of the best-known forms of iconic encoding. Specific icons rich in semantic associations were developed for use with Minspeak™. Using a Minspeak™ strategy, individuals select one, or combine two to three icons, based on their semantic associations, to code messages (Van Tatenhove, 1993).

Beck and Fritz (1998) suggested that Minspeak™ might be an appropriate strategy for persons who have aphasia because it does not require functional literacy skills. Due to the reliance Minspeak™ places on generating and remembering semantic associations, however, Beck and Fritz hypothesized that persons with anterior aphasia would be better able to utilize this strategy than would persons with posterior aphasia. Beck and Fritz (1998) were interested in how the length of the iconic code (i.e., one, two, or three icons) and the abstraction level of the message (i.e., abstract or concrete) would influence competence. They investigated these issues with 10 non-institutionalized participants with aphasia (five with anterior aphasia and relatively preserved comprehension skills and five with posterior aphasia and impaired comprehension skills) and 10 participants without aphasia who had normal communication skills. The participants without aphasia were matched to the participants with aphasia for age, gender, and educational status. All participants were individually taught 24 functional messages coded with Minspeak™ and programmed on an IntroTalker™, a Prentke Romich Company (PRC) AAC device with digitized voice. Of the 24 messages, 12 were abstract and 12 were concrete. For each set of 12 messages, 4 were coded with one icon, 4 with two icons, and the remaining 4 with three icons.

Training consisted of an initial introductory session, three training sessions, one testing session (held on five consecutive days), and a final probe session conducted 1 week after the testing session. In all sessions, each message was preceded by an auditory cue (i.e., "Show me" followed by the exact message) and a visual cue (i.e., a 5 in. × 7 in. colored photograph that related to the message, but did not contain any of the icons used in the message). During the introductory session, the logic for the coding of the message was explained to the participants, the message was modeled for the participant, and the participant was allowed to imitate the production of the message and ask any questions he or she might have. In the training sessions, the participants were required to produce the messages after being given auditory and visual cues. If a participant produced the code correctly, the IntroTalker™ spoke the message, and the experimenter indicated to the participant that the response was correct. If a participant did not produce the code correctly, or did not respond within 30 seconds, the experimenter modeled the code for the participant and asked him or her to imitate the model. In the testing and final probe sessions, participants were required to produce the messages given the auditory and visual cues, but no modeling or feedback (other than the output of the IntroTalker™).

Results of Beck and Fritz's (1998) investigation revealed that persons with aphasia could learn iconic encoding in some conditions. Overall, however, the presence of aphasia had a negative impact on the learning and retention of iconic codes. Furthermore, the abstraction level of the message, length of the iconic code, and type of aphasia also influenced the learning and retention of iconic codes. For all participants, those with and without aphasia, more iconic codes were learned and retained for concrete messages than for abstract messages. All participants learned and retained concrete, one-icon codes at similar levels of high accuracy. Beck and Fritz interpreted this to mean that the participants with aphasia could understand the basic concept of iconic encoding and comprehend the auditory and visual cues used. They indicated that this was consistent with Thorburn et al.'s (1995) results that persons with aphasia were able to comprehend iconic symbols at a level similar to that of persons without aphasia.

Persons with aphasia and high-comprehension skills also learned and retained abstract messages encoded with one icon. Persons with aphasia and low-comprehension skills, however, had more difficulty with this task. Beck and Fritz (1998) suggested that this difference in performance levels between persons with aphasia and high versus low comprehension skills was due to differences in their abilities to know about or to access and use semantic information, especially for abstract messages. This ability is more reduced in persons with posterior aphasias and low-comprehension skills than in persons with anterior aphasias and relatively preserved comprehension skills.

Length of iconic code influenced all participants' abilities to learn and retain codes. As length increased from one to two to three icons, performance for all groups of participants decreased. Again, the performance of persons with aphasia on learning messages of varying icon length was influenced by type of aphasia. Both groups of participants with aphasia (i.e., those with high-comprehension skills and those with low-comprehension skills) were able to learn and retain only a minimal number of codes for concrete messages encoded with three icons and for abstract messages coded with two and three icons. As stated previously, both groups were able to learn and retain one-icon codes for concrete messages. A significant difference in performance between groups of participants with aphasia was shown for learning and retaining two-icon codes for concrete messages: The group of participants with high-comprehension skills learned and retained significantly more of the messages than did the group with low-comprehension skills.

Beck and Fritz (1998) cited differences in the ability to access and utilize semantic information to explain this result. They stated that persons with aphasia and low-comprehension skills "were not able to learn more than one semantic association per message regardless of the abstraction level of the message" (p. 192). These authors suggested that differences in memory and attentional skills could help explain the differences in performance. Some persons with left hemisphere damage and language impairments have been shown to be unable to allocate appropriate resources for both linguistic and visuoperceptual processing tasks, possibly because they are not consciously aware of differences in the linguistic and visuoperceptual complexity of tasks (Clark & Robin, 1995). Furthermore, persons with both frontal and posterior lesions resulting in mild aphasia have demonstrated deficits in attention and resource allocation suggesting that location of lesion is not as important in causing these deficits as is the presence of brain damage (Murray et al., 1997). Beck and Fritz hypothesized that the difficulty all their participants with aphasia demonstrated when trying to learn iconic codes of more than one icon in length could be due to the fact that they did not fully recognize or attend to the difficulty of the task and therefore did not allocate sufficient resources to it. Beck and Fritz reported that their participants with low-comprehension skills had overall lower language scores than did the participants with high-comprehension skills. They suggested that "if attention/resource allocation impairments are due to presence rather than to location of left hemisphere brain damage, then the degree of such impairments may correspond more to the severity level than to the type of aphasia" (p. 193). Therefore, the fact that persons with low-comprehension skills had more difficulty learning one-icon abstract messages and two-icon concrete messages than did persons with high-comprehension skills may also be due, in part, to greater deficits in attention and resource allocation abilities.

Beck and Fritz (1998) concluded that under controlled situations, persons with aphasia are able to learn and retain iconic codes. They cautioned, however, that clinicians must be aware of the "influence on learning of the type of aphasia and associated underlying language and cognitive processes" (p. 193). Implications from their findings regarding message enhancement for persons with aphasia are that persons with aphasia who have good comprehension skills could be candidates for AAC systems using iconic encoding of concrete messages at the one- and two-icon levels and of abstract messages at the one-icon level. Beck and Fritz suggested, however, that longer, more difficult messages should not be presented until persons show success with messages coded at simpler levels. Because Beck and

Fritz's participants who had poor comprehension skills were only able to learn iconic encoding of concrete messages at the one-icon level and because much of the power of Minspeak™ lies with the ability to combine semantic associations, Beck and Fritz suggested that such persons would most likely be better served through the use of a different AAC strategy.

New generations of PRC AAC devices, however, utilize a Minspeak Application Program (MAP) called Unity®. In the beginning level of Unity®, a person selects one icon to express single words. After the person has learned the meanings of single icons, the next levels of Unity® can be utilized in which the person begins building short phrases and complete sentences using the same icons in sequences of two to three icons. It may be that persons with aphasia, especially those with good comprehension skills, may be more easily able to learn iconic encoding using Unity® than the original Minspeak™ encoding system because of its initial use of single icons and gradual introduction of icon sequences.

AAC DEVICES SPECIFICALLY DESIGNED FOR PERSONS WITH APHASIA

Minspeak™, the AAC encoding strategy investigated by Beck and Fritz (1998), was developed for use by persons who have severe communication impairments regardless of the etiology of their impairments. The Talks-Bac™, on the contrary, was developed specifically for use by individuals with nonfluent aphasia (Waller, Dennis, Brodie, & Cairns, 1998). Waller et al. reported that the word-based design of the TalksBac™ resulted from research into the pragmatics of language and utilized a portable MacIntosh PowerBook Duo computer with a 19 × 12-cm plasma screen.

The TalksBac™ has two distinct programs, one for use by the person with aphasia and the other for use by a specified communication partner who programs the device with messages personally relevant to the person with aphasia. The communication partner types in a message and indicates the type of person (e.g., family and friend) with whom the person with aphasia would use the message. The TalksBac™ automatically sets the topic of the message as the first two content words in the message. The partner can add a third topic selection if so desired.

The program provides for a text-based, dynamic display that is accessed with a tracker-ball and button. The first screen a person sees offers a choice of conversational partners (e.g., family, friend, and stranger). When the person has selected the conversational partner, the next screen offers topic choices along the top row and four commonly used sentences, not necessarily related to the topic, underneath these topics (e.g., How are you?). The person can then choose either one of the topics or one of the sentences, in which case the TalksBac™ speaks the sentence using synthesized voice. If a topic is chosen, then four sentences or story titles are displayed. Again, if the person chooses a sentence, it is spoken by the device. If neither the desired topic nor the sentence is displayed, a person can select more buttons that will bring up additional topics and sentences. The TalksBac™ utilizes a predictive feature so that the order in which the topics and sentences are presented to the person with aphasia is determined by the frequency with which the person has previously selected them. In this way, the TalksBac™ is "specific to users, both in the information content and in how it adapts to the individual ways of communicating" (Waller et al., 1998, pp. 49–50).

Waller et al. (1998) tested the use of the TalksBac™ with four participants with nonfluent aphasia. These participants had auditory comprehension skills sufficient to be able to answer yes/no questions accurately and to follow everyday conversation and simple commands allowing them to understand instructions on use of the TalksBac™. Additionally, because the TalksBac™ utilizes a text-based display and is designed to convey informative, interactive messages rather than basic messages, the partici- pants had to possess functional communication and literacy skills. They had sufficient ability to utilize semantic associations so that they could select messages that would be listed under specific partners and topics. They each had a motivated communication partner with whom they had frequent contact who programmed their TalksBac™.

The participants and their communication partners were taught how to use the TalksBac™ in weekly sessions held in the participants' individual homes over the course of 3.5 months. After the training sessions, intervention using the TalksBac™ was conducted for 9 months. To assess the functionality of the TalksBac™ at the end of the 9-month intervention period, four conversations, two with the TalksBac™ and two without, were videotaped for each participant. One conversation with and one conversa- tion without the TalksBac™ were conducted with a familiar conversational partner; the other two conversations were conducted with an unfamiliar partner.

Of the four participants who completed the study, two showed notable improvement in communication when using the TalksBac™ (Waller et al., 1998). Waller et al. reported that a third participant did not use the

TalksBac™ frequently because he had developed other AAC strategies (e.g., use of pictures) to augment his communication that were as effective for him as was the TalksBac™. The fourth participant was unsuccessful in utilizing the TalksBac™ to augment his communication. A fifth participant was unable to complete the study because of the loss of a consistent communication partner. Additionally, it is important to note that the use of case studies, such as these, is considered to be a weak form of evidence (Koul & Corwin, 2003) and so caution must be used in interpreting these results.

The results of Waller et al.'s (1998) investigation of the TalksBac™ indicate that some persons with aphasia who have relatively preserved auditory comprehension and functional communication and literacy skills can learn to utilize a text-based, computerized AAC device. Other persons with the same skill set, however, either were not able to utilize the TalksBac™ or chose to augment communication through other means. This emphasizes the importance of always considering the performance and preference of the person who will be using an AAC system. The success of using the TalksBac™ depended on the availability of a consistent communication partner who could program personally relevant messages and on the frequency of opportunities to utilize the device. These findings underscore the importance of a facilitative environment with motivated and knowledgeable communication partners and opportunities for communication.

Another computer-based AAC device designed specifically for use by people with aphasia is the computer-based visual input communication (C-VIC) system. According to Koul and Corwin (2003), C-VIC has been the system most frequently used by researchers to investigate the ability of people with severe Broca's aphasia or global aphasia to learn to use an AAC system. C-VIC allows persons to construct simple, prepositional phrases and subject–verb–object sentences by dragging icons from a selection of vocabulary items given on the top of the screen to a communication space on the bottom of the screen (Weinrich et al., 1995). Weinrich et al. described the computer screen as including a communication space for clinicians directly above the communication space for clients. The clinician can use this space to provide the client with a template of the desired construction. The communications that are constructed with C-VIC utilize "an unambiguous, simplified syntax which is loosely based on English" (p. 344). All constructions use active voice and have no subordinate clauses. Weinrich et al. indicated that there are no tense markers, articles, declensions, or verb endings and that icons are subdivided and stored in a lexicon as animate nouns, common nouns, verbs, prepositions, and modifiers. Verbs can be animated on the computer screen.

Investigations have consistently indicated that persons with severe aphasia could learn to navigate C-VIC independently (McCall et al., 2000; Weinrich, Boser, & McCall, 1999; Weinrich et al., 1995). Weinrich et al. (1995) and Weinrich et al. (1999) reported that natural speech production of simple sentences by persons with severe aphasia improved after C-VIC training. This improvement was primarily in the directness and the syntactic complexity of productions, not in the phonological form of verbal productions (Weinrich et al., 1995). Weinrich et al. suggested that such improvement could be due to the fact that C-VIC icons remained accessible and visible to the participants while they constructed sentences and that there were only a few possible syntactic frames from which to choose. These aspects of C-VIC may cause its use "to stabilize the activation of appropriate semantic nodes" (p. 361) and to result in a "more rapid selection of a syntactic frame during subsequent verbal production" (p. 361). These factors might allow a person with aphasia to better coordinate the phonological activation of selected lexical nodes with the appropriate slots in the syntactic code and thus improve natural speech production of simple sentence constructions.

McCall et al. (2000) reported results of a case study in which they conducted training sessions over 3 years with a 57-year-old man diagnosed with global aphasia. They reported that with C-VIC, their participant was, after a considerable amount of training, able to select the nouns and verbs that were relevant to a message and able to produce prepositional phrases. He continued, however, to have difficulty producing syntactically correct constructions. Additionally, pretest and posttest measures indicated that training with C-VIC had no significant effects on his natural language comprehension and production.

Koul and Corwin (2003) cited a 1992 study by Weinrich in which results indicated that persons with aphasia have a more difficult time processing C-VIC verbs, even when they were animated, than they do processing C-VIC nouns. Koul and Corwin suggested that "the verb processing deficits seen in individuals with Broca's or global aphasia may transcend the modality (i.e., visual/verbal) in which symbols are presented" (p. 455).

Koul and Harding (1998) conducted a study to evaluate the ability of persons with severe or global aphasia to comprehend and produce graphic symbols with the Talking Screen™ (TS) by Words+, a commercially available software system that was not designed specifically for individuals with aphasia. Koul and Harding found that their participants learned to operate a computer, navigate through the software system, and use nouns more easily than verbs. Koul and Harding suggested that superior performance with nouns might be due to the fact that nouns are more iconic than verbs. To explain the ability of persons with aphasia to learn a computer-based graphic symbol system, Koul and Harding cited the facts that both the TS and the C-VIC rely on recognition memory as opposed to phonetic processing and that vocabulary items are presented in a systematic manner that provides cues for selection.

The implications of Koul and Harding's (1998) results and the results of investigations with C-VIC (e.g., McCall et al., 2000; Weinrich et al., 1995, 1999) are that even persons with severe Broca's aphasia or global aphasia can benefit from the use of a computerized graphic AAC system that utilizes simple sentence structures and that provides structured presentations of stimuli that rely on recognition memory. Clinicians should recognize, however, that learning verbs may take more time and training than learning nouns even if the abstraction level of verbs is decreased through animation.

These positive implications are somewhat dampened by the fact that the performance of persons with aphasia in C-VIC studies and in Koul and Harding's (1998) study was so variable that no predictions could be made regarding how an individual person with severe aphasia would perform on computer-based AAC systems. Additionally, little evidence has been reported indicating that the use of such systems increase the functional or interactive communication of individuals with aphasia (Jacobs et al., 2004), and most of the data regarding the effectiveness of C-VIC are based on case studies, considered to be weak forms of evidence (Koul & Corwin, 2003).

Lingraphica® is a commercially available AAC device that utilizes icons and that was developed based on the research conducted on C-VIC (McCall et al., 2000). Illustrations of the Lingraphica® and videos of its use by persons with aphasia can be found on Lingraphica®'s web site. Harris, Shireman, and Steele (1997) reported that Lingraphica® has gone through multiple revisions and refinements since the basic C-VIC technology was acquired by LingraphiCARE America in 1990–1991. Lingraphica® is a portable, flexible system that contains more than 5,000 manipulable graphic icons covering the primary parts of speech. Lingraphica® also contains self-documenting capabilities that run in the background and keep records of the extent to which the Lingraphica® is utilized. The latest version of the Lingraphica®, Version 7, allows a person to customize the device using the built-in camera to create personalized icons and videos (Lingraphica® the Aphasia Company™).

Harris et al. (1997) described an overall treatment plan in which the use of Lingraphica® was one component. Treatment was provided in community-based programs formally designated as Language Care Center Programs. Other components of the program included a patient care algorithm, a specially designed database, and highly trained and qualified speech–language pathologists. The patient care algorithm took into account each client's medical etiology, speech–language pathology diagnosis, severity level, response to treatment, and individual goals. The algorithm then supplied a framework for individualized treatment plans and materials to be used in treatment. The database tracked clients' performance throughout treatment at a Language Care Center Program so that client progress could be monitored in a timely and effective manner. Speech–language pathologists were trained to understand and appropriately utilize the algorithm, database, and Lingraphica®. Lingraphica® was programmed by speech–language pathologists to be appropriate for each client's level and rate of progress. It was used in both one-on-one sessions at the centers and by the clients at home. Harris et al. reported that Lingraphica's self-documenting capabilities indicated that clients used their devices more than 2 hours daily in treatment activities, which, these authors concluded, indicated a high level of motivation.

Aftonomos et al. (2001) reported an outcome study of 50 clients who were assessed before and after treatment at two Language Care Center Programs. Pretest and posttest assessments included standardized diagnostic tests administered by certified speech–language pathologists and standardized functional communication tests completed by family members. The clients participated in individual, 50-minute treatment sessions with speech–language pathologists and were given home programs to follow. The mean number of treatment sessions clients participated in was 37.8. Overall, clients' mean scores on both the diagnostic tests and the functional communication tests showed significant improvement from pretest to posttest. However, further analysis revealed that improvement patterns after treatment vary depending on whether the participants are classified based on diagnostic test scores or based on functional communication test scores.

Aftonomos et al. (2001) explained that this study was not a controlled experimental study and that their data therefore "do not support the drawing of further conclusions regarding, for example, absolute efficacy, comparative efficacy, or attribution of causality" (p. 961). Additionally, they indicated that the persons who participated were referred to Language Care Center Programs by others who believed that they could benefit from participation in the therapy program. A participant sample bias may have existed. Aftonomos et al. argue, however, that their participant sample broadly mirrored the population of other community-based therapy programs. Aftonomos et al. (2001) cited another potential source of bias: Neither the speech–language pathologists who administered the diagnostic tests nor the family members who completed the functional communication tests were blinded as to the purpose of the study.

Despite these cautions, however, Aftonomos et al. (2001) concluded that their report documenting significant improvement on both diagnostic tests and functional communication tests for persons with both chronic and acute aphasia in both controlled and naturalistic settings is noteworthy. As these authors pointed out, the results are especially important given the skepticism in the medical community as to the value of speech–language therapy for persons with severe aphasia and reports of lack of carryover into functional settings.

It has not been determined exactly how the use of Lingraphica contributed to the improvement in clients' communication skills. Factors such as structured one-on-one sessions designed and continually monitored by highly trained speech–language pathologists, the portability of the AAC device, the reportedly high at-home use (i.e., 2 hours a day) of the device, and the involvement of family members are key factors that may help to ensure success (and thereby message enhancement) with many different devices. Nonetheless, taken together with results of previous C-VIC studies, the results of Aftonomos et al.'s (2001) outcome study do indicate that the potential "intuitive fit between AAC and persons with severe aphasia" (p. 1238) suggested by Jacobs et al. (2004) should continue to be studied and pursued.

A recent development is the use of apps for small platform mobile technologies. Favorite icons, phrases, and videos on the Lingraphica® can be synchronized with iPod Touches and iPhones by transferring these favorites to Lingraphica®'s Small Talk Aphasia app for iPhones and iPod Touches (Lingraphica® the Aphasia Company™, n.d.). These new apps present exciting new communication possibilities for persons with aphasia, and their use is an area that demands further study.

Another fairly current development in the area of AAC technologies for use with persons with aphasia is the use of visual scene displays (VSDs). A research team at the University of Nebraska, in collaboration with colleagues from Penn State University and engineers from DynaVox Technologies, developed a prototype device that utilizes VSDs specifically for use by persons with aphasia (Blackstone, 2004; Dietz et al., 2006). The prototype emphasized the communicative functions associated with social interactions and exchange of information rather than expression of needs and wants (Blackstone, 2004). As Blackstone indicates, the ability to engage in social interactions utilizing small talk, telling stories, discussing world events, gossiping about friends and family, and so on is critical because these topics are the basis of many adult interactions, and being unable to engage in these types of conversations can cause a person's social circles to shrink and put him or her at risk for increasing isolation.

According to Blackstone (2004), the goal of the Nebraska project was "to develop a prototype device that (1) uses digital images (scenes) to represent meaning, (2) enables people with aphasia to navigate from scene to scene during a conversation and (3) reduces the cognitive and linguistic load of using AAC technology" (p. 9). The digital images used are photos or pictures that represent experiences, places, or situations of personal significance for the person with aphasia (Dietz et al., 2006). These photos and pictures are accompanied by text and symbols to "(1) support specific content (e.g., names, places), (2) cue communication partners about questions or topics that are supported by displays and/or (3) support navigation features" (Blackstone, 2004, p. 10).

The digital images are typically in the center of the device screen. As Blackstone (2004) describes this form of a VSD, the images are not "hot spots" on the device screen. That is, if a person touches them, the device is not activated. In this way, the person can use the images as they would a photo album. Blackstone reports that the work done by the Nebraska team indicated that it is important for these first pictures to be highly personal and rich enough in context to support at least five conversational turns. Around the images are buttons that allow the person to speak messages, ask questions, or navigate more deeply into a theme with supplementary images that could be more generic than the first images and that provide more specific and detailed information about the theme. The VSD can also contain smaller images around the periphery that when activated shift the screen to a different topic of discussion.

Blackstone (2004) observed that when language representation and categorization tasks are reduced in complexity, people with severe aphasia have been able to navigate through the system utilizing impressive visuospatial skills. She stated that "VSDs allow individuals with aphasia to make use of their strengths with images, to navigate through pages of content and to communicate in ways that cannot be accomplished using low-tech communication book applications and current AAC technologies" (p. 12).

A significant part of the apparent success of VSDs in allowing persons with aphasia to participate in social interactions is the very personal and highly contextual nature of the VSDs. According to Dietz et al. (2006), there are three phases of the total programming of a VSD: the informant phase, the programming phase, and the validation phase. Before the informant phase, the family and the person with aphasia are asked to provide relevant pictures to the clinician. The clinician then downloads or scans digital pictures into a computer editing program. During the informant phase, a meeting or several meetings if needed are held with the clinician, family members or a caregiver, and the person with aphasia in which the individual pictures are discussed to determine details about and themes around each picture. The clinician summarizes his or her perception of the themes for each picture, and the other members at the meeting confirm or correct.

During the programming phase, the VSDs are created using photos representing each theme. "The photos within a theme are then systematically programmed to correspond with the key ideas related to the theme that were expressed during the informant phase" and "the key ideas are provided as written text" (Dietz et al., 2006, p. 16). At this point, the programmed theme is downloaded into a device. The final phase is the validation phase. The person with aphasia reviews the themes providing input as to accuracy and acceptability.

Researchers at the Augmentative and Alternative Communication-Rehabilitation Engineering Research Center and DynaVox® Technologies (n.d.) have developed high-technology devices, specifically the V™ and the Vmax™, that offer VSDs (Blackstone, 2007; DynaVox® Technologies). At this time, low-technology versions of VSDs are also available at no cost from the University of Nebraska, Lincoln web site. The use of personally relevant, contextualized photographs, such as those used in VSDs, has been found to allow people with severe aphasia to be more successful in processing information than when the information "appears in other forms that convey less contextualized information or have less personal relevance" (McKelvey et al., 2010, p. 32). Hux, Buechter, Wallace, and Weissling (2010) also reported that the use of low-technology VSDs improved the ability of a person with aphasia to communicate with unfamiliar conversational partners.

Although the data to date that support the use of high-technology VSDs come from only a few case histories, they do appear to be promising. They enhance messages for people with aphasia by utilizing highly personal and contextualized images that encourage social interactions and coconstruction of messages with communication partners. Additionally, VSDs rely heavily on visuospatial skills that are typically preserved in persons with severe aphasia while minimizing the cognitive and linguistic load associated with the use of other AAC technologies.

CONCLUSIONS

The results of the studies cited in this chapter indicate that persons with aphasia can use AAC technologies to enhance messages for functional communication. Several key factors appear to be important (see Table 1). Individual strengths, weaknesses, preferences, and interests must be considered. A carefully structured approach to intervention designed by qualified speech–language pathologists that considers these factors, designs intervention based on them, carefully monitors progress, adjusts intervention to match progress made, and incorporates both one-on-one sessions and home practice results in improvements in functional communication. Some persons, however, choose AAC options to facilitate their communication that do not include technology. This choice must be honored.

While type and severity of aphasia likely influence a person's ability to use an AAC device, in general, AAC devices that present simplified and personally relevant messages and depend on recognition memory appear to be those that are learned most successfully and used most functionally. A key criterion for the functional use of a device is portability that affords the flexibility of use at home as well as out in the community. Newly developed communication apps for mobile technologies will increase this critical portability aspect. Because apps are such a new area of possibility for persons with aphasia, however, little research has been done regarding whether and how apps will ultimately facilitate the communication abilities of people with aphasia. This research must be done to ensure appropriate use of this technology.

Finally, supportive communication partners who are integral partners in planning the content and organization of content programmed into a device and who accept, support, and encourage the use of AAC by the person with aphasia must be involved in the implementation of AAC. This involvement is vital to ensuring that the use of AAC results in the overall goal of enabling individuals to interact with others in their environments and to thereby increase their participation in activities of daily life.

Table 1. Summary of AAC Studies with Implications for Message Enhancement.

Authors	AAC Strategy	Implications for Message Enhancement
Beck and Fritz (1998)	Iconic encoding – not designed specifically for persons with aphasia	Type of aphasia influences performance. Persons with good comprehension skills can learn and retain two-icon sequences for concrete messages; persons with low-comprehension skills do not learn sequences. Abstraction level influences performance: Concrete messages are learned and retained better than abstract messages. Length influences performance: As length increases, performance decreases
Waller et al. (1998)	TalksBac™ – designed specifically for persons with aphasia	Some persons with aphasia and relatively preserved comprehension skills, functional communication, and literacy skills can learn to use a text-based, computerized AAC device. Individual abilities and preferences along with the presence of facilitative communication environments, with supportive communication partners are important for positive outcomes
McCall et al. (2000) Weinrich et al., 1995Weinrich et al. (1999)	C-VIC – designed specifically for persons with aphasia	Persons with aphasia can learn to navigate system independently. System helps improve natural language skills for some individuals; verbs are more difficult for some to process than other word classes
Koul & Harding, 1998	Commercially available graphic software – not specifically designed for persons with aphasia	Persons with severe aphasia can learn to use graphic systems that utilize simple sentence structures and depend on use of recognition memory. Verbs may be more difficult to learn than other word classes
Aftonomos et al. (2001)	Lingraphica® – designed from C-VIC specifically for people with aphasia	Persons with aphasia of all severity levels improved both on standardized diagnostic tests and on functional communication tests after therapy utilizing Lingraphica® in one-on-one sessions designed, provided, and continually monitored by qualified speech–language pathologists and in home sessions involving family members
Nebraska project as reported by Blackstone (2004) and Dietz et al. (2006)	Prototypes of VSDs – designed for specific persons with aphasia	People with aphasia increased involvement in social interactions utilizing highly personal and contextualized images that allow for coconstruction of messages with communicative partners

REFERENCES

Aftonomos, L., Steele, R., Appelbaum, J., & Harris, V. (2001). Relationships between impairment-level assessments and functional-level assessments in aphasia. *Aphasiology*, *15*, 951–964.

Beck, A., & Fritz, H. (1998). Can people who have aphasia learn iconic codes? *Augmentative and Alternative Communication*, *14*, 184–196.

Beukelman, D., Ball, L., & Fager, S. (2008). An AAC personal framework: Adults with acquired complex communication needs. *Augmentative and Alternative Communication*, *24*, 255–267.

Beukelman, D., Fager, S., Ball, L., & Dietz, A. (2007). AAC for adults with acquired neurological conditions: A review. *Augmentative and Alternative Communication*, *23*, 230–242.

Beukelman, D., & Mirenda, P. (2005). *Augmentative and alternative communication: Supporting children and adults with complex communication needs* (3rd ed.). Baltimore, MD: Paul H. Brooks.

Blackstone, S. (2004). Adults with aphasia. *Augmentative Communication News*, *16*, 9–12.

Blackstone, S. (2006). Adults with acquired disabilities. *Augmentative Communication News*, *18*, 4–6.

Blackstone, S. (2007). AAC technologies for adults with aphasia and traumatic brain injury. *Augmentative Communication News*, *19*, 6–7.

Clark, H., & Robin, D. (1995). Sense of effort during a lexical decision task: Resource allocation deficits following brain damage. *American Journal of Speech-Language Pathology*, *4*, 143–147.

Darley, F. L. (1982). *Aphasia*. Philadelphia, PA: W. B. Saunders.

Dietz, A., McKelvey, M., & Beukelman, D. (2006). Visual scene displays (VSD): AAC interfaces for person with aphasia. *Perspectives on Augmentative and Alternative Communication*, *15*(1), 13–17.

DynaVox Technologies. (n.d.). *Possible AAC solutions for stroke survivors*. Retrieved from http://www.dynavoxtech.com/start//stroke/solutioins.aspx. Accessed on March 11, 2011.

Garrett, K., & Lasker, J. (2005). Adults with severe aphasia. In: D. Beukelman & P. Mirenda (Eds.), *Augmentative and alternative communication: Supporting children and adults with complex communication needs* (3rd ed., pp. 467–504). Baltimore, MD: Paul H. Brooks.

Goodglass, H., & Baker, E. (1976). Semantic field, naming, and auditory comprehension in aphasia. *Brain and Language*, *3*, 359–374.

Grober, E., Perecman, E., Kellar, L., & Brown, J. (1980). Lexical knowledge in anterior and posterior aphasics. *Brain and Language*, *10*, 318–330.

Harris, V., Shireman, C., & Steele, R. (1997). Under managed care; Innovative programming for adults with aphasia. *Advance Online Edition*. Retrieved from http://speech-language-pathology-audiology.advanceweb.com/common/EditorialSearch/AViewer.aspx?AN=SP_p9.html&AD = 06-09-1997. Accessed on 13 June 2006.

Hux, K., Buechter, M., Wallace, S., & Weissling, K. (2010). Using visual scene displays to create a shared communication space for a person with aphasia. *Aphasiology*, *24*(5), 643–660.

Hux, K., Manasse, N., Weiss, A., & Beukelman, D. (2001). Augmentative and alternative communication for persons with aphasia. In: R. Chapey (Ed.), *Language intervention strategies in aphasia and related neurogenic communication disorders* (4th ed., pp. 675–687). Philadelphia, PA: Lippincott Williams & Wilkins.

Jacobs, B., Drew, R., Ogletree, B., & Pierce, K. (2004). Augmentative and alternative communication (AAC) for adults with severe aphasia: Where we stand and how we can go further. *Disability and Rehabilitation, 26*, 1231–1240.

Koul, R., & Corwin, M. (2003). Efficacy of AAC intervention in individuals with chronic severe aphasia. In: R. Schlosser (Ed.), *The efficacy of augmentative and alternative communication*, (pp. 449–470). Amsterdam: Academic Press.

Koul, R., & Harding, R. (1998). Identification and production of graphic symbols by individuals with aphasia: Efficacy of a software application. *Augmentative and Alternative Communication, 14*, 11–23.

Koul, R., & Lloyd, L. (1998). Comparison of graphic symbol learning in individuals with aphasia and right hemisphere brain damage. *Brain and Language, 62*, 394–421.

Kraat, A. (1990). Augmentative and alternative communication: Does it have a future in aphasia rehabilitation? *Aphasiology, 4*, 321–338.

Lingraphica® the Aphasia Company™. (n.d.). Lingraphica®. Retrieved from http://www.aphasia.com/slp/product_features.aspx. Accessed on March 11, 2011.

McCall, D., Shelton, J., Weinrich, M., & Cox, D. (2000). The utility of computerized visual communication for improving natural language in chronic global aphasia: Implications for approaches to treatment in global aphasia. *Aphasiology, 14*, 795–826.

McKelvey, M., Hux, K., Dietz, A., & Beukelman, D. (2010). Impact of personal relevance and contextualization on word-picture matching by people with aphasia. *American Journal of Speech-Language Pathology, 19*, 22–33.

McNeil, M. (1983). Aphasia: Neurological considerations. *Topics in Language Disorders, 3*, 1–19.

McNeil, M., & Kimelman, M. (2001). Darley and the nature of aphasia: The defining and classifying controversies. *Aphasiology, 15*, 221–229.

Murray, L., Holland, A., & Beeson, P. (1997). Auditory processing in individuals with mild aphasia: A study of resource allocation. *Journal of Speech, Language, and Hearing Research, 40*, 792–808.

Thorburn, L., Newhoff, M., & Rubin, S. (1995). Ability of subjects with aphasia to visually analyze written language, pantomime, and iconographic symbols. *American Journal of Speech-Language Pathology, 4*, 174–179.

Van Tatenhove, G. (1993). *What is Minspeak?* Wooster, OH: Prentke Romich Co.

Waller, A., Dennis, F., Brodie, J., & Cairns, A. (1998). Evaluating the use of the TalksBac, a predictive communication device for nonfluent adults with aphasia. *International Journal of Language and Communication Disorders, 33*, 45–70.

Weinrich, M., Boser, K. I., & McCall, D. (1999). Representation of linguistic rules in the brain: Evidence from training an aphasic patient to produce past tense verb morphology. *Brain and Language, 70*, 144–158.

Weinrich, M., McCall, D., Weber, C., Thomas, K., & Thornburg, L. (1995). Training on an iconic communication system for severe aphasia can improve natural language production. *Aphasiology, 9*, 343–364.

CHAPTER 7

WHAT DO SOCIAL VALIDATION DATA TELL US ABOUT AAC INTERVENTIONS?

Ralf W. Schlosser

INTRODUCTION

In 1999, Lapointe, Katz, and Braden noted that "results of a few studies that address social validation have begun to appear in the literature such as ..., but for the most part social validation of change in aphasic performance is conspicuous by its absence" (p. 788). Twelve years later, there are more social validation reports available, but an informal look at the approximate rate of such studies per year does not seem to have moved forward the overall rate to any substantial degree. Hence, the purpose of this chapter is to introduce the reader to the AAC Social Validation Matrix to (1) stimulate aphasia researchers to conduct more intervention studies that include social validation, (2) motivate practitioners to seek out social validation data when examining the evidence base for a particular intervention as part of evidence-based decision making, and (3) encourage practitioners to collect their own practice-based social validity data related to the clients on their caseloads.

Augmentative and Alternative Communication for Adults with Aphasia
Augmentative and Alternative Communications Perspectives, Volume 3, 115–127
ISSN: 2047-0991/doi:10.1108/S2047-0991(2011)0000003013

WHAT IS SOCIAL VALIDATION AND WHY SHOULD WE CARE?

Social validation is the process of assessing the social significance of interventions (Kazdin, 2011; Wolf, 1978). Social validation is one of the cornerstones of applied behavior analysis, but has found its way into other related fields including communication disorders in general (Goldstein, 1990) and the field of augmentative and alternative communication in particular (Schlosser, 1999, 2003). While objective data that establish a causal relation between an intervention and outcome measures continues to be paramount to documenting the effectiveness of an intervention, the construct of social validity has focused attention on the perspectives of those who experience the intervention. Additionally, the advent of evidence-based practice (EBP) has further elevated the importance of the perspectives of relevant stakeholders. Namely, "relevant stakeholder perspectives" is one of three aspects involved in the EBP process that has to be integrated with research evidence and clinical expertise in the decision-making process (Schlosser & Raghavendra, 2004). As noted by Schlosser (2003), "the availability of favorable social validation data serves as a distinguishing criterion that helps separate an effective treatment with social validity from another effective treatment without social validity" (p. 224). Presumably, when relevant stakeholders in an intervention study deem the intervention to be successful, the stakeholders involved in the decision-making process relative to a person with aphasia (PWA) are more likely to find this intervention to be socially valid as well. In particular with a population where interventions often rely on communication partner training, social validation appears to have a lot to offer; after all, these partners would like to see the PWA to be successful.

THE AAC SOCIAL VALIDATION FRAMEWORK

Schlosser (1999) proposed a conceptual framework to assist clinicians and researchers to socially validate interventions in AAC. The framework includes three main components: (a) How: methods (subjective evaluation, social comparison); (b) Who: stakeholder perspectives or performance (direct, indirect, immediate community, extended community); and (c) What: intervention components (goals, methods, outcomes).

The *"How"* Component

The "How" component refers to the groups of methods employed for gathering social validation data. In principle, two broad categories of methods are distinguished. One is called *subjective evaluation* and the other is referred to as *social comparison* (Wolf, 1978).

Subjective Evaluation

Subjective evaluation involves the soliciting of opinions and perspectives of individuals who (a) are directly or indirectly affected by an intervention, (b) have experience with an intervention, and/or (c) control the feasibility of an intervention. Specific methods to elicit these perspectives may include questionnaires and structured or unstructured interviews. In terms of questionnaires, the usage rating profile-intervention (URP-I) (Chafouleas, Briesch, Riley-Tillman, & McCoach, 2009), for example, allows interventionists to assess acceptability, feasibility, and understanding of the intervention. The URP-I is a 35-item questionnaire that uses a 6-point Likert rating scale with strong evidence of internal consistency and construct validity. Interviews are often conducted in conjunction with questionnaires and Likert-type scales because they permit more open-ended type of assessments, particularly when the interview is unstructured. Another means of assessing treatment acceptability is the Treatment Evaluation Inventory-Short Form (TEI-SF), a nine-item survey with strong evidence of internal consistency (Kelley, Heffer, Gresham, & Elliott, 1989) and validity (Njardvik & Kelley, 2008). In the AAC intervention literature for individuals with aphasia, the following instruments have been used as part of subjective evaluation efforts (see Aftonomos, Steele, Appelbaum, & Harris, 2001; Corwin, Koul, & Zens, 2005; Ribitzki, 2003; Steele, Aftonomos, & Koul, 2010; Zens, 2005): the Communication Readiness and Use Index, the Psychosocial Well-Being Index (Lyon et al., 1997), the Communicative Effectiveness Index (Lomas et al., 1989), and the Program Evaluation Inventory, which is a modified version of the TEI-SF. For details on these applications to individuals with aphasia as well as the use of interviews, the reader is referred to Chapter 8.

Social Comparison

Social comparison refers to a group of methods that evaluate the comparability of stakeholder performance before or after the intervention with a group of individuals whose behavior is considered to be "typical," "desirable," or "normal" (Epstein & Cullinan, 1979; Kazdin & Matson, 1981). As such, social comparison data cannot be obtained from the targeted individual with aphasia or those who may indirectly benefit from the intervention this individual receives. Therefore, one of the key issues an interventionist has to address pertains to the selection of the comparison group. Schlosser (1999) discussed the pros and cons of using typical individuals versus successful individuals with disabilities. The argument has been made that it is often more meaningful to compare the targeted individuals' performance with other individuals who have the same disability (here aphasia) but who are considered successful communicators. This decision, however, depends on the specific intervention context at hand. For example, if the context is competitive employment it may be appropriate to compare performance of an individual with aphasia to that of nondisabled peers. In other contexts (e.g., interactions with family), it may be appropriate to select individuals who use AAC successfully as a comparison group. Goldstein (1990) points out that the gathering of social comparison data should be an experimental process, whereby the interventionist carefully matches the comparison group on selected characteristics (individuals who function well despite disabilities) to the clinical group, while avoiding overlap with the clinical population. Social comparison data are decidedly not about perspectives of relevant stakeholders, but about objective performance. In sum, social comparison data can inform the interventionist whether the level of performance attained by a PWA is comparable to nondisabled individuals or other PWA who are considered successful communicators.

The "Who" Component

The "Who" component is the next logical component to address. For subjective evaluation efforts, whose perspectives should be solicited? There is some agreement in the field that those stakeholders should be included whom directly or indirectly control the feasibility of an intervention (Fawcett, 1991). Schlosser (1999) proposed that the AAC field adopt the taxonomy of consumers proposed for the field of applied behavior analysis by Schwartz and Baer (1991) while replacing the term "consumer" with the term "stakeholder" to yield the following four types: (1) direct stakeholders, (2) indirect stakeholders, (3) immediate community stakeholders, and (4) extended community stakeholders.

For the purposes of this chapter, direct stakeholders typically are the PWA who are receiving AAC interventions. Given that successful AAC interventions with this population often require communication partner training (Koul & Corwin, 2003), the spouses or paid caregivers could be the direct stakeholders for such interventions. Indirect stakeholders may be affected by any outcomes yielded by the direct stakeholder and, as such, may indirectly influence the feasibility of interventions. This could involve spouses or other family members of the PWA. Immediate community stakeholders regularly interact with direct or indirect stakeholders either socially or professionally. This includes friends, extended family members, or paid caregivers such as nurses or physician assistants. Extended community stakeholders do not interact with the direct and indirect stakeholders on a regular basis and may or may not know them. They could be, for example, a waiter in the restaurant in which the PWA likes to eat. Others are clinicians and researchers in the field of AAC. The reason that extended community stakeholders might control the feasibility of an intervention is because those situations require the PWA to interact with unfamiliar communication partners.

For the group of methods referred to as "social comparison," the selection of relevant stakeholders has been already addressed, in part, earlier. To recap, social comparison cannot involve direct stakeholders or indirect stakeholders. However, social comparison samples could involve immediate community stakeholders or extended community stakeholders.

The "What" Component

The third component of the social validation matrix involves decisions as to what aspect of the intervention can and should be socially validated. There are three aspects worthy of socially validating, including (1) goals, (2) methods, and (3) outcomes.

Goal Validation

According to Fuqua and Schwade (1986), goals may be validated in terms of their *topography* and/or the *level*. Topography is another term for the form of communicative behaviors and involves broad social goals, behavioral categories, and discrete responses. Schlosser (1999) defined and exemplified these topographies for AAC: broad social goals are considered the value base that underlies AAC; that is, the desire to teach PWAs to attain communicative competence (Light, 1989). Behavioral categories are the hypothesized sub-categories of the broad social goals and include operational, strategic, linguistic, and/or social competence. Finally, for discrete responses there are specific behaviors that make up the behavioral categories such as switching between different modalities to accommodate listener knowledge and experience. The topography of goals may be assessed by means of subjective evaluation of relevant stakeholder perspectives or through social comparison. By socially validating goal topography by means of subjective evaluation, the interventionist increases the likelihood that the goals that are eventually targeted are acceptable to those that are directly or indirectly involved in the intervention (e.g., the PWA and/or his spouse and other family). This, in turn, may result in better buy-in and compliance with the implementation of the intervention. Assessing the goal topography through subjective evaluation may also increase the goodness-of-fit between the intervention and the setting and communication partners. Assessing goal topography through social comparison ensures that the topographies that are eventually targeted are indeed used or can be used by PWA who are considered successful communicators. Ogletree, Howell, and Carpenter (2005) have developed a systematic procedure for setting socially valid goals based on the work of others and this chapter's author. The procedure includes (1) fact finding with direct and indirect stakeholders, (2) external validation through comparison interviews with extended community stakeholders, and (3) collaborative problem solving and goal prioritization through brainstorming. Readers may consult this reference for further guidance on this process; in addition to describing process, Ogletree and colleagues offer an illustrative case example.

Besides validating the topography of a goal, the interventionist may also assess the level of validation. The level of validation is essentially concerned with the anticipated outcomes; however, this assessment occurs before beginning an intervention. If the interventionist relies on goal attainment scaling for goal setting and outcome monitoring (e.g., Schlosser, 2004), goal level validation would entail a process that involves relevant stakeholders in arriving at operational definitions of the expected level of performance (0), the better than expected outcome (+1), the best expected outcome (+2), the worse than expected outcome (−1), and the worst expected outcome (−2). If the interventionist uses more traditional goal setting, goal validation may involve an assessment to arrive at a definition as to when criterion is reached (e.g., 80% correct in three consecutive sessions).

Methods Validation
Besides goals, the interventionist may also wish to socially validate the methods. This includes the materials that are being used as well as the procedures. According to Schlosser (1999), "the validation of intervention

materials may include articles that are used during all screening, baseline, or implementation phases of a given intervention, including equipment (e.g., communication devices), overlays, symbols, words, story boards, and videotapes" (p. 242). It is conceivable that an interventionist would ask a PWA and/or their caregivers to rate the graphic symbols they propose to use on a speech generating device using a Likert scale that is appropriate for the individual. For example, a Likert scale could be used with only 3-point rating levels (agree, undecided, disagree) and/or using pictorial differentials (e.g., Engell, Hütter, Willmes, & Huber, 2003) instead of the typical 7-point or 5-point rating scales without pictorial differentials. This would allow the interventionist to determine whether these symbols are deemed appropriate for this given individual before deciding on the symbols that would be ultimately used.

In addition to materials, methods validation may entail the procedures to be used. According to Kazdin (1980), procedure validation entails the validation of the *type* and *form* of intervention. Fawcett (1991) proposed that the type of procedures could be validated at three levels; however, these levels seem more relevant to service delivery models or practices rather than specific interventions per se. In terms of type, the interventionist could elicit input from relevant stakeholders on whether the planned intervention is worthy of pursuing. For example, in an evaluation of the written choice communication strategy (see Lasker, Hux, Garrett, Moncrief, & Eischeid, 1997), the investigators could have assessed the social validity of this type of intervention in general and in the two formats which they compared to one another.

Based on Schlosser (1999), the validation of the form "may address any specific procedural detail for the intervention selected including the length of pauses, type of strategies used, and the type of feedback provided" (p. 242). AAC interventions in aphasia could, for example, validate the latency at which the PWA has to respond or initiate within a communication exchange. Here, indirect stakeholders may be most suitable when using subjective evaluation or successful PWAs when using social comparison.

Outcomes Validation
Besides goals and methods, social validation efforts may also target outcomes. There is no better quote than that of Wolf (1978) regarding the social validation of outcomes:

> Are consumers satisfied with the results, all of the results [positive or negative], including those that were unplanned? Behavioral treatment programs are designed to help

someone with a problem. Whether or not the program is helpful can be evaluated only by the consumer. Behavior analysts may give their opinions, and these opinions may even be supported with empirical objective behavioral data, but it is the participants and other consumers who want to make the final decision about whether a program helped solve their problems. (p. 210)

To date, the majority of social validation efforts in the aphasia intervention literature has been concerned with the social validation of outcomes (e.g., Corwin et al., 2005; Cupit, Rochon, Leonard, & Laird, 2010; Doyle, Goldstein, & Bourgeois, 1987; Hickey & Rondeau, 2005; Jacobs, 2001; Lapointe, Katz, & Braden, 1999; Lustig & Tompkins, 2002; Massaro & Tompkins, 1994; Ribitzki, 2003; Steele et al., 2010; Zens, 2005) relative to the validation of goals or methods. This work has yielded some interesting findings, some of which are briefly summarized as follows (the findings pertaining directly to AAC are discussed in Chapter 8).

Lustig and Tompkins (2002) taught a PWA and apraxia of speech to use a self-initiated written word when a protracted articulatory struggle occurred across three settings. The intervention was found effective in objective terms and also yielded favorable social validation ratings of shorter videotaped segments (not longer ones) by unfamiliar raters comprised primarily of graduate students in speech-language pathology and audiology (i.e., extended community stakeholders). Lapointe et al. (1999) selected a large sample of community members diverse in age, education, and occupation (i.e., extended community stakeholders) to judge the accuracy of changes in writing samples from PWA, as a result of intervention. The unfamiliar raters were able to detect the changes observed through quantitative means. Cupit et al. (2010) examined whether extended community stakeholders (speech-language pathologists, young laypersons, older laypersons) noticed a difference following naming treatment of 11 PWA (7 of who received treatment). Results indicated that all three groups of raters noticed the changes in those PWA that received treatment, and perhaps more importantly, did not notice any change in those PWA that were not treated. Interestingly, the raters' different levels of experience with PWA did not seem to affect their ability to detect changes.

In each of the above studies, the social validity of outcomes supported the outcomes obtained through objective means. Therefore, these interventions are not only effective, but they also appear to be noticed as such by relevant stakeholders; that is, they are socially valid.

To assist interventionists with outcome validation, Schlosser (1999), based on previous work of the author and others, proposed the following outcomes classification for the social validation of AAC interventions:

(1) proximal, (2) instrumental, (3) intermediate, and (4) distal. Proximal outcomes are perceived changes that are directly related to the intervention. If, for example, the goal of intervention is for the PWA to maintain a social interaction, proximal outcome validation is concerned with how relevant stakeholders (subjective evaluation) rate the PWA's performance in maintaining conversations as a result of intervention or how successful PWA compare in terms of this skill to the targeted PWA (social comparison).

Instrumental outcomes are perceived changes presumed to lead to other outcomes without further intervention. For example, the improved use of partner-focused questions by individuals using AAC may lead to improved overall communicative competence. In an investigation by Light, Binger, Agate, and Ramsey (1999), 20 individuals without AAC experience (i.e., extended community stakeholders) were asked to rate the communicative competence of individuals using AAC before and subsequent to intervention on asking partner-focused questions.

Intermediate outcomes are perceived changes in total "quality of life" as a result of AAC intervention. While more and more studies are being conducted that examine various aspects of quality of life of PWA (e.g., Cranfill & Wright, 2010; Hilari & Byng, 2009; Manders, Dammekens, Leemans, & Michiels, 2010), these are typically not occurring as part of an intervention study. As such, while important for the field, these efforts have not moved into the arena of social validation. Clearly, there is a critical issue in need of further study.

Distal outcomes are perceived changes for stakeholders as a group. As such, they require large-scale studies with representative samples of the population of PWA who use AAC. To date, to the knowledge of this author, such efforts are not yet available.

THE MEASUREMENT OF SOCIAL VALIDATION

In terms of methodology and measurement, social validation data should be collected with the same degree of rigor toward minimizing threats to internal validity as is done for the intervention under investigation (Schlosser, 2003). This includes the careful selection of relevant stakeholders or the comparison group, the selection of questionnaires and survey instruments that bear construct validity or predictive validity, the collection of reliability data for social comparison data, and careful consideration of the time between treatment and administering social validation assessments. In terms of the latter, for example, in the absence of a pretest of stakeholder acceptability of an impending intervention, it is tedious to attribute a positive evaluation to that intervention if it occurs only after the intervention; it is difficulty to rule out that it was a preformed opinion that existed beforehand. Instead, it is preferred to map the social validation design onto the experimental design used to demonstrate treatment efficacy (see Schlosser, 2003; Storey & Horner, 1991). For further information on the measurement of social validation, including a checklist for appraising the certainty of social validation evidence, the reader may wish to consult Schlosser (2003).

SUMMARY

The reader was introduced to the AAC social validation matrix to communicate the importance of three main components of social validation: (1) the how, (2) the who, and (3) the what. Social validation, as a construct and as a set of methods, has great potential to help AAC intervention with PWA find its heart (to paraphrase a statement made by Wolf, 1978, for the field of applied behavior analysis). As of yet, this potential has not been fully realized. It is the hope of this author that this chapter will stimulate more AAC intervention research with PWA that involves social validation. A similar call has been made by Jacobs, Drew, Ogletree, and Pierce (2004), who asked investigators to "carefully examine their methods, goals, and outcome measure to determine their social validity" (p. 238). Furthermore, hopefully this chapter will encourage practitioners to ask for the social validity of AAC interventions with this population. Finally, this chapter may lead more practitioners to collect social validity data in their daily practice.

REFERENCES

Aftonomos, L., Steele, R., Appelbaum, J., & Harris, V. (2001). Relationships between impairment-level assessments and functional-level assessments in aphasia. *Aphasiology*, *15*, 951–964.

Chafouleas, S. M., Briesch, A. M., Riley-Tillman, T. C., & McCoach, D. B. (2009). Moving beyond assessment of treatment acceptability: An examination of the factor structure of the usage rating profile-intervention (URP-I). *School Psychology Quarterly*, *24*, 36–47.

Corwin, M., Koul, R. K., & Zens, C. (2005). Communication skills training for caregivers of persons with severe aphasia. Paper presented at the Annual Speech-Language and Hearing Association convention, San Diego, USA.

Cranfill, T. B., & Wright, H. (2010). Importance of health-related quality of life for persons with aphasia, their significant others, and SLPs: Who do we ask? *Aphasiology, 24,* 957–968.

Cupit, J., Rochon, E., Leonard, C., & Laird, L. (2010). Social validation as a measure of improvement after aphasia treatment: Its usefulness and influencing factors. *Aphasiology, 24,* 1486–1500.

Doyle, P. J., Goldstein, H., & Bourgeois, M. S. (1987). Experimental analysis of syntax training in Broca's aphasia: A generalization and social validation study. *Journal of Speech and Hearing Disorders, 52,* 143–155.

Engell, B., Hütter, B., Willmes, K., & Huber, W. (2003). Quality of life in aphasia: Validation of a pictorial self-rating procedure. *Aphasiology, 17,* 383–396.

Epstein, M. H., & Cullinan, D. (1979). Social validation: Use of normative peer data to evaluate LD interventions. *Learning Disabilities Quarterly, 2,* 93–98.

Fawcett, S. B. (1991). Social validity: A note on methodology. *Journal of Applied Behavior Analysis, 24,* 235–239.

Fuqua, R. W., & Schwade, J. (1986). Social validation of applied behavioral research: A selective review and critique. In: A. D. Poling & R. W. Fuqua (Eds.), *Research methods in applied behavior analysis* (pp. 265–292). New York, NY: Plenum.

Goldstein, H. (1990). Assessing clinical significance. In: L. B. Olswang, C. K. Thompson, S. F. Warren & N. J. Minghetti (Eds.), *Treatment efficacy research in communication disorders. Proceedings of the American Speech-Language-Hearing Foundation's national conference on treatment efficacy* (pp. 91–98). San Antonio, TX: ASHA.

Hickey, E., & Rondeau, G. (2005). Social validation in aphasiology: Does judges' knowledge of aphasiology matter? *Aphasiology, 19,* 389–398.

Hilari, K., & Byng, S. (2009). Health-related quality of life in people with severe aphasia. *International Journal of Language & Communication Disorders, 44,* 193–205.

Jacobs, B. B., Drew, R. R., Ogletree, B. T., & Pierce, K. K. (2004). Augmentative and alternative communication (AAC) for adults with severe aphasia: Where we stand and how we can go further. *Disability & Rehabilitation, 26,* 1231–1240.

Jacobs, B. J. (2001). Social validity of changes in informativeness and efficiency of aphasic discourse following linguistic specific treatment (LST). *Brain and Language, 78,* 115–127.

Kazdin, A. E. (1980). Acceptability of alternative treatments for deviant child behavior. *Journal of Applied Behavior Analysis, 13,* 259–273.

Kazdin, A. E. (2011). *Single-case research designs: Methods for clinical and applied settings* (2nd ed.). New York, NY: Oxford University Press.

Kazdin, A. E., & Matson, J. L. (1981). Social validation in mental retardation. *Applied Research in Mental Retardation, 2,* 39–53.

Kelley, M. L., Heffer, R. W., Gresham, F. M., & Elliott, S. N. (1989). Development of a modified treatment evaluation inventory. *Journal of Psychopathology and Behavioral Assessment, 11,* 235–247.

Koul, R., & Corwin, M. (2003). Efficacy of augmentative and alternative communication intervention in individuals with chronic severe aphasia. In: R. W. Schlosser, *The efficacy of augmentative and alternative communication: Toward evidence-based practice* (pp. 449–470). New York, NY: Academic Press.

Lapointe, L. L., Katz, R. C., & Braden, C. L. (1999). Clinical significance of change in language performance: Social validation of writing response improvement in aphasia. *Aphasiology, 13,* 787–792.

Lasker, J., Hux, K., Garrett, K., Moncrief, E., & Eischeid, T. (1997). Variations on the written choice communication strategy for individuals with severe aphasia. *Augmentative and Alternative Communication, 13*, 108–116.

Light, J. (1989). Toward a definition of communicative competence for individuals using augmentative and alternative communication systems. *Augmentative and Alternative Communication, 5*, 137–144.

Light, J., Binger, C., Agate, T. L., & Ramsey, K. N. (1999). Teaching partner-focused questions to individuals who use augmentative and alternative communication to enhance their communicative competence. *Journal of Speech and Hearing Research, 42*, 251–255.

Lomas, J., Pickard, L., Bester, S., Elbard, H., Finlayson, A., & Zoghaib, C. (1989). The communicative effectiveness index: Development and psychometric evaluation of a functional communication measure for adult aphasia. *Journal of Speech and Hearing Disorders, 54*, 113–124.

Lustig, A. P., & Tompkins, C. A. (2002). A written communication strategy for a speaker with aphasia and apraxia of speech: Treatment outcomes and social validity. *Aphasiology, 16*, 505–521.

Lyon, J. G., Cariski, D., Keisler, L., Rosenbek, J., Levine, R., Kumpula, J., ... Blanc, M. (1997). Communication partners: Enhancing participation in life and communication for adults with aphasia in natural settings. *Aphasiology, 11*, 693–708.

Manders, E. E., Dammekens, E. E., Leemans, I. I., & Michiels, K. K. (2010). Evaluation of quality of life in people with aphasia using a Dutch version of the SAQOL-39. *Disability and Rehabilitation: An International, Multidisciplinary Journal, 32*, 173–182.

Massaro, M., & Tompkins, C. (1994). Feature analysis for treatment of communication disorders in traumatically brain-injured patients: An efficacy study. In: M. L. Lemme (Ed.), *Clinical aphasiology* (Vol. 22, pp. 245–256). Austin, TX: Pro-Ed.

Njardvik, U., & Kelley, M. L. (2008). Cultural effects on treatment acceptability: A comparison of the acceptability of behavioral interventions between Icelandic and American parents. *Nordic Psychology, 60*, 283–294.

Ogletree, B. T., Howell, A., & Carpenter, D. (2005). A procedure for socially valid goal setting. *Intervention in School and Clinic, 41*, 76–81.

Ribitzki, T. (2003). *Efficacy of computer-based voice output communication intervention in persons with chronic severe aphasia.* Unpublished master's thesis. Texas Tech University Health Sciences Center, Lubbock, TX.

Schlosser, R. W. (1999). Social validation of interventions in augmentative and alternative communication. *Augmentative and Alternative Communication, 15*, 234–247.

Schlosser, R. W. (2003). Determining the social validity of AAC interventions. In: R. W. Schlosser, *The efficacy of augmentative and alternative communication: Toward evidence-based practice* (pp. 203–228). San Diego, CA: Academic Press.

Schlosser, R. W. (2004). Goal attainment scaling as a clinical measurement technique in communication disorders: A critical review. *Journal of Communication Disorders, 37*, 217–239.

Schlosser, R. W., & Raghavendra, P. (2004). Evidence-based practice in augmentative and alternative communication. *Augmentative and Alternative Communication, 20*, 1–21.

Schwartz, I. S., & Baer, D. M. (1991). Social validity assessments: Is current practice state of the art? *Journal of Applied Behavior Analysis, 24*, 189–204.

Steele, R., Aftonomos, & Koul, R. (2010). Outcome improvements in persons with chronic global aphasia following the use of a speech-generating device. *Acta Neuropsychologica, 8,* 342–350.

Storey, K., & Horner, R. H. (1991). An evaluative review of social validation research involving persons with handicaps. *The Journal of Special Education, 25,* 352–401.

Wolf, M. M. (1978). Social validity: The case for subjective measurement, or how applied behavior analysis is finding its heart. *Journal of Applied Behavior Analysis, 11,* 203–214.

Zens, C. (2005). *Effects of caregiver training and AAC intervention on facilitating communication skills of individuals with aphasia.* Unpublished master's thesis. Texas Tech University Health Sciences Center, Lubbock, TX.

CHAPTER 8

SOCIAL VALIDATION OF AUGMENTATIVE AND ALTERNATIVE COMMUNICATION INTERVENTIONS IN APHASIA

Melinda Corwin

INTRODUCTION

When deciding whether a particular intervention is effective and efficient, one important but often-overlooked aspect to consider is how the persons involved in the intervention felt about it. Often referred to as *stakeholders*, these are the individuals who experience the intervention either directly or indirectly (Schlosser, 2003). In the case of augmentative and alternative communication (AAC) intervention and aphasia, persons with aphasia (PWA) are the direct stakeholders. Indirect stakeholders include persons who are strongly affected by the intervention (e.g., close family members). Immediate community stakeholders include persons who regularly interact on a social or professional level with direct or indirect stakeholders (e.g., extended family members, close friends, facility staff members, and hired caregivers). Extended community stakeholders include persons in the community who rarely or never interact with the direct and indirect stakeholders (e.g., civic or retail personnel) or experts in the field of AAC/ aphasia (e.g., clinicians and researchers).

Augmentative and Alternative Communication for Adults with Aphasia
Augmentative and Alternative Communications Perspectives, Volume 3, 129–154
Copyright © 2011 by Emerald Group Publishing Limited
All rights of reproduction in any form reserved
ISSN: 2047-0991/doi:10.1108/S2047-0991(2011)0000003014

When evaluating the effectiveness of a particular intervention, the social significance of the intervention goals, methods, and outcomes must be considered (Schlosser, 2003). In other words, the intervention must be socially valid. If an intervention is found to be socially invalid, it fails to facilitate target behavior in a meaningful and useful way and is not likely to be used successfully over the long term by direct or indirect stakeholders. Standardized tests alone provide limited information on spontaneous, functional interactions of PWA (Lomas et al., 1989; Manochiopinig, Sheard, & Reed, 1992; Murray & Chapey, 2001). The use of social validity measures reveals improvements that are unnoticed by standardized measures (Boles, 1998). As Schlosser (2003) stated, "stakeholders' perspectives on the outcomes attained are of vital importance in any science involved with human behavior" (p. 204). Social validation provides information about whether or not a particular intervention makes a meaningful difference in the lives of PWA and those around them. Goals of treatment, methods for obtaining the goals, and results (outcomes) must be socially acceptable to those directly and indirectly experiencing the intervention. If this occurs, the intervention is more likely to be used.

The process of social validation involves conducting subjective evaluations as well as social comparisons for the intervention in question (Schlosser, 2003). Subjective evaluations of the intervention should come from all of the different stakeholders. Pre- and postintervention assessments could be in the form of questionnaires, rating scales, interviews, and/or direct observations. The stakeholders' perceptions and opinions about the intervention goals, methods, and outcomes are considered. Social comparisons of the intervention are conducted by comparing the communicative performance of PWA to the performance of persons without aphasia, or by comparing the communicative performance of PWA who use a particular form of AAC versus the performance of PWA who do not use the same particular form of AAC. Measures of social comparison could be completed by comparing the two groups via experiments, observations during communication tasks, and/or outcome behaviors (Schlosser, 2003).

As the provision of speech-generating devices (SGDs) becomes more widespread, a question arises: Is the AAC intervention program involving the use of an SGD valued by indirect stakeholders? Indirect stakeholders are the people who will be interacting with the person using the SGD, so their role in determining its importance and usefulness is essential. This proposition does not intend to detract from standardized and quantitative measures, but it does expose the problems of using those techniques in isolation.

Light (1989) defined *communicative competence* as the capacity to communicate functionally in the natural environment and to sufficiently meet communication needs on a daily basis. Lyon et al. (1997) studied 10 PWA and volunteer communication partners who were trained to use a list of communication strategies during conversational interactions and community outings. The researchers used a combination of standardized (formal tests), nonstandardized (questionnaires), and informal (subjective ratings) measures to evaluate pre- and posttreatment differences in the PWA. The results indicated a lack of improvement when the 10 PWA were evaluated using standardized measures. Despite this, statistically significant ($p < 0.05$) improvements were noted on nonstandardized measures (questionnaires) in the areas of well-being and overall communication. This outcome led the authors to propose that standardized measures as they are used now may not truly report the achievements of PWA due to the measures' lack of sensitivity and specificity. Instead of or in addition to using standardized measures, criterion-referenced measures may be more sensitive. Social validation measures may also detect perceived changes that are not captured by standardized or criterion-referenced measures because stakeholders will assess the intervention from their perspectives, reporting on issues that are important to them.

For a clinician, the goal of treatment is to provide an intervention that will be generalized to situations outside of the therapy room. Developing an intervention program that is perceived to provide improvement for an individual will not matter unless it can be shown that the individual will apply the program in daily life. A social validation analogy is provided in the following scenario: If you were to ask a person to try a new razor that involves a series of painful electric shocks, the razor may work wonderfully in terms of removing unwanted hair; however, if the person perceives the razor as painful and cumbersome to use, s/he will not use it, despite it being an objectively *valid* way to remove unwanted hair. Similarly, PWA (direct stakeholders), their close family members (indirect stakeholders), and others in their daily environment (immediate community stakeholders) may be asked to establish intervention goals and methods that are incongruent with their intentions or desires. This could result in outcomes for the stakeholders that are less-than-ideal or even undesirable.

It is critical to seek opinions from all of the stakeholders in a variety of ways to determine whether or not a particular intervention is truly successful. This chapter will explore some of the possible ways to investigate the perspectives and opinions of stakeholders. Actual examples of research studies incorporating these investigations are provided when possible.

INVESTIGATING SOCIAL VALIDATION

Previous studies have demonstrated that PWA have the ability to use SGDs in experimental settings (e.g., Koul & Corwin, 2003; Koul & Harding, 1998; Koul, Corwin, & Hayes, 2005); however, few studies have examined whether or not this type of intervention is a socially valid one for PWA or other stakeholders (e.g., Ribitzki, 2003; Zens, 2005). To determine whether or not the AAC intervention using a SGD was considered socially valid by the PWA as well as their caregivers, Ribitzki (2003) completed a study which involved both quantitative and qualitative methodology. Data were collected in the forms of structured conversation analysis as well as rating scales from PWA and their caregivers. The study involved nine individuals with severe Broca's or global aphasia (six females and three males) who were trained to use a GUS© AAC graphic symbol system that had been downloaded to a Dell Inspiron 4000 laptop computer. This SGD provided a means of communication between the PWA and their caregivers. Selection of appropriate messages/vocabulary items for a particular participant depended on the information provided by the caregivers as well as the participant's linguistic, motor, and sensory capabilities. Thus, each participant had his or her own customized SGD. The participants selected symbols with the aid of a touch screen, which resulted in production of words or phrases in a synthetic voice. A male synthetic voice was used for male participants, and a female synthetic voice was used for female participants. A related study (Zens, 2005) included a caregiver training component, which involved training the tenets of Supported Conversation for Adults with Aphasia (SCA™) (Kagan, 1995) in addition to the use of an SGD with PWA. Some caregivers were family members (e.g., significant other, daughter), whereas others were paid staff (e.g., certified nursing aide). Pre- and postintervention data were collected by asking PWA as well as caregivers to complete rating scales. Finally, while working on this book chapter, this author completed preliminary qualitative analyses of interview transcripts obtained from caregivers, which provided additional information regarding the caregivers' perspectives and opinions regarding the AAC intervention using an SGD. In sum, three different types of data were obtained from two different sources (structured conversational analysis of PWA, rating scales from PWA and caregivers, and semi-structured interviews of caregivers) to inform socially valid practices for improving communication between PWA and those with whom they interact. These three methods of investigation and analysis are described in the following sections, along with results.

STRUCTURED CONVERSATION ANALYSIS

Conversation analysis has been used by some researchers (e.g., Damico, Oelschlaeger, & Simmons-Mackie, 1999; Goodwin, 1995; Oelschlaeger & Thorne, 1999) to examine communication in situations that are closer to everyday life rather than traditional therapy dialogue between PWA and clinicians, which is often more didactic in nature (Simmons-Mackie, 2008). In the Ribitzki (2003) study, clinicians asked PWA to engage in conversation on preselected topics. The clinicians served as conversational partners and initiated conversation by using designated closed and open-ended questions/statements that were specifically chosen for each preselected topic. The conversation partners were instructed to follow the PWA's lead during and after stating the designated questions, and to continue or discontinue the conversation as appropriate.

The conversational samples were transcribed and analyzed using the following three dependent variables: (1) overall effectiveness of communication (i.e., percentage of effective responses compared to percentage of ineffective responses), (2) percentage of the number of times the SGD was used as a mode to communicate information, and (3) percentage of the number of times modes of communication other than the SGD (i.e., verbal, nonverbal, vocalization, or no response) were used during interactions.

The modes of communication were operationally defined in order to minimize overlap. If the participant communicated by using the SGD, resulting in synthetic speech output, this was coded as "SGD." If the participant communicated by using speech, this was coded as "S" for speech. If the participant communicated by using techniques that did not involve speech such as gestures, pointing, head nodding/shaking, and writing, this was coded as "NV" for nonverbal. Nonverbal communication included selecting arrows to move to a different computer screen or deleting a previously selected item because these selections did not result in synthetic speech output. Also, if the participant pointed to something on the computer but did not select it (i.e., no synthetic speech was generated), it was also coded as "NV." If the participant communicated by producing sounds without intelligible speech, this was coded as "VO" for vocalization.

The participant's communication turns were judged to be effective/ successful (coded as "EF") if participation in the conversation was any of the following:

1. Appropriate (i.e., suitable, valid, and acceptable)
2. Adequate (i.e., sufficiently answered the question)
3. Relevant (i.e., applicable and related)

The participant's communication turns were judged to be ineffective/ unsuccessful (coded as "IE") if participation in the conversation was any of the following:

1. Inappropriate (i.e., awkward)
2. Inadequate (i.e., ambiguous or invalid effort to respond)
3. Irrelevant (i.e., not logical; response showed no understanding of the question/statement)

If the veracity of the participant's comments or responses could not be confirmed but the conversational turn was appropriate, the turn was coded as "EF" for effective. For example, if the experimenter asked how many days the participant was in the hospital and the participant responded with "40," this was judged as effective because it was an appropriate answer, whether or not it was actually true. Examining the statements that preceded and followed the communication turn was also an important factor in determining whether or not the communication turn was effective.

One of nine possible codes could be assigned on a conversational turn. In the paragraphs that follow, actual examples of each of these codes will be provided. For clarification purposes, note that regular font type indicates speech used by the PWA; bold-faced type indicates SGD symbol selection by the PWA, resulting in synthetic speech output; italic type indicates vocalizations, such as laughing or moaning; and information typed in parentheses indicates other nonverbal forms of communication, such as pointing or gesturing.

The code "SGDEF" was used if the participant communicated by using the SGD (resulting in synthetic speech output) and communication was effective. This is illustrated by the following example:

Conversational partner: Tell me about your past job.
Participant with aphasia: *Robertson's Floral Shoppe*

The code "SGDIE" was used if the participant communicated by using the SGD (resulting in synthetic speech output) and communication was ineffective. This is illustrated by the following example:

> Conversational partner: Can you tell me why Halloween is your favorite holiday?
> Participant with aphasia: *Halloween.*

The code "SEF" was used if the participant communicated by using spoken words and communication was effective, as illustrated by the following example:

> Conversational partner: Do you collect anything?
> Participant with aphasia: Yeah.

The code "SIE" was used if the participant communicated by using spoken words and communication was ineffective. This included the use of automatic phrases, such as "Good heavens" or "Let me see," and unintelligible utterances. The following is an example of SIE:

> Conversational partner: What do you like to do with your family?
> Participant with aphasia: Sower.

The code "NVEF" was used if the participant communicated by using techniques that did not involve speech and communication was effective. This is illustrated by the following example:

> Conversational partner: What is your personality like?
> Participant with aphasia: (Pointed to the word *friendly* on the computer screen.)

The code "NVIE" was used if the participant communicated by using techniques that did not involve speech and communication was ineffective. If the transcript stated that the participant searched for a response but never found one or gave the experimenter a blank or questioning look, this was judged as NVIE because interpretation of underlying intent was too subjective/unclear (e.g., the PWA could have been communicating the need for help, thinking about an unrelated topic, attempting to but unsuccessfully expressing a concept, or expressing frustration). The following is an example of NVIE:

Conversational partner: Tell me how you feel when you paint.
Participant with aphasia: (Shook hand in the air.)

The code "VOEF" was used if the participant communicated by producing sounds and communication was effective, as illustrated by the following example:

Conversational partner: I'm sure she always does what she's told.
Participant with aphasia: *(Laughed.)*

The code "VOIE" was used if the participant communicated by producing sounds and communication was ineffective, as illustrated by the following example:

Conversational partner: What is your favorite movie?
Participant with aphasia: *(Moaned.)*

The code "NRIE" was used if the participant offered no response, which was always coded as ineffective. This included attempts to verbalize which resulted in a failed communicative attempt. The following is an example of NRIE:

Conversational partner: Where did you go?
Participant with aphasia: [Attempted to verbalize.]

At times, the participants responded with a combination of communication modes, such as selecting an item on the SGD while speaking aloud. When this happened, the response was coded with the mode of communication that was considered to be the primary or main way the message was communicated. The following example would be coded "SGDEF" because the participant mainly communicated the message via the SGD, even though the participant used both SGD and oral (spoken) modes of communication:

Conversational partner: Who came to your house for lunch?
Participant with aphasia: *Mom. Dad.* Hey, I know. *Parents.*

Once the entire conversational transcript data had been coded as described in the previous paragraphs, Ribitzki (2003) conducted an analysis of variance (ANOVA). Results of a 2×5 ANOVA indicated a significant main effect for mode $[F_{(4, 99)} = 4.434, p < 0.01]$ and effectiveness $[F_{(1, 99)} = 17.91, p < 0.01]$. Additionally, the main effect for mode was modified by a significant two-way interaction between mode and effectiveness $[F_{(4, 99)} = 6.08, p < 0.01]$. Across modes, use of the SGD had higher effective responses (mean = 30.5) than other modes of communication (verbal mean = 27.6; nonverbal mean = 21.8; vocalization mean = 1.0; and no response = 0). Results revealed that the most frequently used mode of communication was a SGD, followed by verbal, nonverbal, and vocalization. Additionally, most of the communication attempts across modes were effective (mean = 16.18) more than ineffective (mean = 4.56). Analyses using post-hoc Newman–Keuls ($p < 0.05$) revealed the following: The effective responses were significantly higher than the ineffective responses across all modes except vocalization. The SGD mode was used a significantly greater mean number of times than vocalization. There was no significant difference between the mean number of times the SGD mode and verbal mode were used for communication. In sum, PWA used a combination of SGD, verbal, and nonverbal modes to communicate in an overall effective manner with conversational partners.

Conversational analysis can provide a basis for comparing communication characteristics of PWA and communication characteristics of persons without aphasia. In terms of social comparisons, PWA may use an SGD to serve the same function during conversation as persons without aphasia who use speech. Although this particular study did not involve conversational samples from a social comparison control group of individuals without aphasia, it provides some initial data regarding performance of PWA. If PWA use a SGD to perform better during conversational interactions compared to PWA who do not use a SGD, we can begin to hypothesize that AAC intervention using a SGD is socially valid.

RATING SCALES

Quantitative rating scales contain a high linguistic code, which require the individuals using them to have intact memory and comprehension. As a result of intact right hemisphere function following left hemisphere brain lesions, PWA have a tendency to identify pictures and line drawings with greater ease than written words (Gainotti, Silveri, & Sena, 1989; Goldstein, Canavan, & Polkey, 1988; Koul & Corwin, 2003; Koul & Lloyd, 1998; Wapner & Gardner, 1981). Thus, modifications to quantitative scales should be made for PWA to ensure that the scales are more easily understood.

Research indicates that visual analogue scales are sensitive instruments and clearly reflect changes over time (Bond & Lader, 1974; Lomas et al., 1989). The visual analogue scale, a validated self-report measure, usually consists of a 10-cm line on paper with verbal anchors labeling the ends (Collins, Moore, & McQuay, 1997; Ferraz et al., 1990; Harms-Ringdahl et al., 1986; Price, McGrath, Rafii, & Buckingham, 1983). Soh and Ang (1992) found that they are particularly useful for populations with language barriers, as indicated by their study which compared pain rating scales among cancer patients that only spoke Chinese. Using visual analogue scales to rate subjective feelings was employed as early as 1921 by Hayes and Patterson when it was referred to as the graphic rating scale. The following advantages of this scale were listed by Freyd (1923): The graphic rating scale is easily understood by participants, quickly completed and scored, and barely requires participant motivation. Additionally, this format does not require knowledge of quantitative terms (i.e., 1, 2, 3, etc.), thus making it more conducive for obtaining subjective measurements from PWA. Recent measures such as the *Assessment for Living with Aphasia* (Kagan et al., 2010), *Communication Quality of Life Scale (ASHA CQL)* (Paul et al., 2004), and a pictorial/written version of the *Aachen Life Quality Inventory* (Engell, Hutter, Willmes, & Huber, 2003) have also successfully employed visual analogue scales for PWA.

Zens (2005) attempted to measure social validity by collecting data from two sets of participants (PWA and their caregivers) regarding whether or not an AAC program involving SGD intervention for PWA and direct conversational training for caregivers employed acceptable treatment goals and procedures, and whether or not the participants experienced satisfaction with the overall program. Two rating scales (i.e., the Communication Readiness and Use Index (CRUI) and the Psychosocial Well-Being Index (PWI)) (Lyon et al., 1997) were administered to 15 PWA and one scale (i.e., the Communicative Effectiveness Index (CETI)) (Lomas et al., 1989) was administered to 15 caregivers. Additionally, the Program Evaluation Inventory (PEI), a modified version of the Treatment Evaluation Inventory (TEI) (Kelley, Heffer, Gresham, & Elliot, 1989), was administered to both sets of participants after the AAC (SGD + Caregiver Training) intervention. The response format of the scales for PWA was changed to a visual analogue format. Each visual analogue scale consisted of vertical lines measuring 10 cm (100 mm), except for the CETI, which consisted of horizontal lines. Vertical (rather than horizontal) lines were helpful for the participants with aphasia because some of them had visual field deficits or neglect that interfered with their ability to locate printed items on the left side of a horizontal line. The CETI, which was only administered to the caregivers, was designed with a horizontal line visual analogue scale as there was no need for vertical lines. An example of one PWA's marking on a scale item (at three different points in time) is provided in Fig. 1.

The PWA were required to make a mark on the scale with polar opposites of a target measure at the two ends of the scale. For example, one of the questions in the CRUI is "How 'confident' are you that you'll be able to tell a family member/friend what you want?" The polar opposites of this question are "very confident" and "not at all confident." The informed condition technique was used to collect data across scales. This technique allowed the participants to *calibrate* themselves by referring to their preintervention responses and accurately providing their postintervention opinions regarding whether or not they noted a change or felt differently at the conclusion of the intervention experience. The CRUI and the PWI were completed by the PWA before and after AAC (SGD + Caregiver Training) intervention. The CETI was completed by the caregiver before and after intervention. The PEI was completed by the PWA and the caregivers after intervention.

Pre- and posttest scores from each scale were compared. Results revealed no statistically significant differences ($p > 0.05$) between the mean scores on any of the scales. Although not statistically significant, the difference across questions on the CRUI pre- (mean = 34.75) and postintervention

2. Very Content

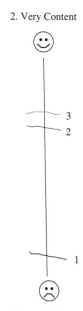

Not at All Content

Fig. 1. Example Rating by Person with Aphasia at Pre- (Labeled as 1), During- (Labeled as 2), and Post- (Labeled as 3) AAC Intervention Points on the Following Item from the CRUI: "How Comfortable are You in Communicating with a Stranger?"

(mean = 41.08) was substantial, indicating that participants found AAC (SGD + Caregiver Training) intervention to be effective. The PEI was administered to both the PWA and caregivers after the intervention to determine if they believed that the program employed acceptable treatment procedures and goals, and if they felt overall satisfaction with the intervention program. On a 100-point scale, the mean scores for PWA across 7 questions ranged from 82.2 to 88.3. The mean scores for caregivers across 7 questions ranged from 82.9 to 92.3. In summary, the mean data for PWA and caregivers indicated that they were very satisfied with the AAC intervention program, and visual analogue rating scales seem to be helpful for assessing the social validity of particular intervention programs. These rating scales can be used to gather and evaluate opinions from several different stakeholders.

STRUCTURED INTERVIEWS

As stated in Chapter 4, the ability of PWA to use alternative forms of communication outside structured treatment contexts has been limited and may be due, at least in part, to inadequate emphasis on communication partner training. Further, lack of generalization data is a considerable problem. Beck and Fritz (1998), Garrett and Lasker (2005), Koul and Harding (1998), Koul et al. (2005), Lasker, Garrett, and Fox (2007), McCall, Shelton, Weinrich, and Cox (2000), and Shelton, Weinrich, McCall, and Cox (1996) observed that in order to make computer-based AAC intervention more effective for PWA, the communication partners must be trained to use strategies that can facilitate communication of PWA. Simply replacing natural language with a graphic symbol, manual sign, or a computer-based AAC system will not facilitate the functional communication skills of individuals with severe or global aphasia (Koul & Corwin, 2003). A key component in the effectiveness of AAC intervention is ensuring that the communication partners without aphasia are secure and accustomed to the communication modes employed by their partner with aphasia.

In addition to training PWA on the use of an SGD, caregivers in the Zens (2005) study were explicitly trained regarding the use of the SGD as well as other facilitative/supportive conversation techniques. Two instructional videos entitled *Supported Conversation for Aphasic Adults* (Kagan, Winckel & Shumway, 1996) and *Treating Aphasia Outside the Clinic* (American Speech-Language-Hearing Association (ASHA), 1998) were viewed by the PWA and caregiver participants. Caregiver participants also received a copy of the *Examples of Facilitative and Non-facilitative Communication Strategies*, adapted from Florance (1981) and Kagan (1998).

Each caregiver in the Zens (2005) study participated in three structured interviews at the following times: before AAC intervention, during intervention (approximately 2–4 weeks after intervention had begun), and after completion of the intervention. The interview questions were constructed with the intent to promote open-ended discussion regarding the meaning of aphasia in the lives of the caregivers as well as helpful and nonhelpful means or strategies for communicating/interacting. Because a semi-structured interview format was used, the questions served as a guide rather than a formal schedule. The interviewer first established rapport with the caregiver participant and followed his or her lead in an attempt to gain temporary access to his or her psychological and social world. General interview questions included the following:

1. Please describe a typical situation where you are talking with [your relative/the resident].
   a. Probe – Tell me more about what (your relative/the resident) was trying to say.
2. Describe a situation where talking with (your relative/the resident) was fairly easy for you.
3. Describe a situation where talking with (your relative/the resident) was fairly hard for you.
4. Do you have any special techniques/strategies for helping to communicate with or talk with (your relative/the resident) when communication was fairly hard for you?
   a. Describe a situation where your strategies seemed to work best.
   b. Describe a situation where no matter what you did, it did not work.
5. Describe a time when you were trying to talk with (your relative/the resident) but you just could not get your idea across.
6. Describe a time when you were trying to talk with (your relative/the resident) but you just could not figure out what (your relative/the resident) was trying to say.
7. Describe a situation where you could not go as deep into your discussion as you wanted to.
   a. What about when you were trying to express your feelings?
8. (Time 1) You are going to learn how to use a computer when talking with (your relative/the resident). Do you have any concerns about learning how to use this computer?
   a. Please describe any situation where you found using a computer particularly challenging.
   b. Please describe any situation where you found using a computer to be particularly helpful or rewarding.
9. (Time 2) You have been learning how to use a computer when talking with (your relative/the resident). Do you have any concerns about using this computer?
   a. Please describe any situation where you found using a computer particularly challenging.
   b. Please describe any situation where you found using a computer to be particularly helpful or rewarding.
   c. Describe your most successful use of the computer with (your relative/the resident).

10. Is there anything else that you would like to tell me about that I have not asked?

Following verbatim transcription of each audio-taped interview, this author conducted extensive qualitative analyses using guidelines from Kendall, Hatton, Beckett, and Leo (2003): This author read each transcript several times and made notes using key words in the margins. She then attempted to identify overall themes, categories, and/or concept clusters within each participant's transcript. Results have not yet been published. Preliminary findings are described in the following paragraphs.

Before AAC intervention (SGD + caregiver training program), caregivers were asked about their modes of communication and their feelings when interacting with their partners with aphasia. Overall themes identified during the qualitative analysis were feelings of frustration and limitation in terms of communication with the PWA. Caregivers reported that communication occurred only at a basic level, mainly regarding daily routines rather than complex, abstract, and/or emotional concepts. An excerpt from one caregiver who was a significant other living at home with her partner with aphasia is provided below. Note that transcripts were typed verbatim to capture the actual words used, and ellipses indicate pauses lasting >2 s. Contextual, nonverbal information is included in brackets.

> Well, we don't sit down and just talk. Pretty much I pick the topics or there's something urgent or that we need to discuss like menus for the day or ... whether or not the dishes are done or similar kind of basic kinds of things. We don't just talk about emotions or ... I tell her sometimes what's happened during my day and sometimes, like, if I tell her one night... sometimes she can remember the next day what happened and sometimes she can't ... so, there's not a lot of carryover sometimes. Um ... we don't really discuss anything particularly ...

A paid caregiver at an assisted living facility described communication with the resident with aphasia as follows:

> Most of the time it is very frustrating because he's trying to tell me something and I don't understand. Sometimes he can get the word out.

If he can give me a one-word clue, I can go from there. You know, if you just have an area to start with … If you just don't have a clue, then it's … you've got the whole world to think about [laugh]. But, most of the time, it's pretty frustrating. And he's gotten better. At first it was just horrible [laugh] because it was just so hard. But he's gotten better with, the…okay, he can't say it … just stop for a minute … and you tell him, "Just rest a minute and think about it." And sometimes he'll just come up with a word or two that will give me a clue and I can just kind of go from there, because if he says, "Go," I'll find out if he wants to go somewhere. And I can ask him, "Where?" and he can either point in a direction, or sometimes he will say, "Street" … down the street, or something. And you just kind of go from there …

By carefully examining and reviewing the interview transcripts, important information regarding the caregivers' feelings of frustration/limitation as well as actual problems that arose during interactions were revealed. Additionally, this author observed that family members and staff members understandably had somewhat different agendas for their interactions: Family members were more interested in talking about deeper, more emotional issues; whereas, staff members were more interested in resolving communication difficulties involving the person's immediate needs.

To determine if caregivers' feelings and opinions changed as a result of the AAC intervention (SGD + caregiver training), this author conducted a preliminary analysis of postintervention interview transcripts. Caregivers expressed positive differences and changed perspectives as a result of the SGD and communication strategies training. They also identified helpful strategies for facilitating communication. The most frequently mentioned beneficial strategies included the use of wait time/patience, appropriate questions, specific prompts, humor, and familiar routines.

One caregiver (significant other) conveyed the benefits of the following supported conversation strategies: wait time, appropriate closed and open-ended questions, and appropriate verbal cueing in the form of cloze procedures. The following is an excerpt from the interview:

The one that I've really been practicing on is when I lead [PWA] into a topic or to a sentence. She already … like … "Today for lunch you had …" And I just wait and let her finish the sentence. And that one has been the hardest one for me, so I need to practice on that one. The pausing is another one that I have a hard time with. We have to pause for 30 seconds and I tend to ... if you don't say it right away I jump in with whatever I think is right and that just confuses her. It takes a little bit longer ... Before the study, I really tended to use 'yes' and 'no' questions and didn't anticipate that [PWA] would come back with anything. And now I know that if I wait, she can come out with whole sentences sometimes or if I set it up, like "For lunch you had ..." then she can say, "Grilled cheese sandwich with ..." whatever it is and she comes out with her whole thought. And I've tried that also with her when she's stuck on a sentence. Like, her mom told her something over the phone the other day and we were having ... She wanted to tell me what she had told her, but every time she tried to say it, her mouth would make something different than what she wanted it to make. And so, I tried to set it up like, "Your mother told you on the phone about ..." and she finished the sentence. It was easier ... or seemed to be. It took a few false starts, but it was a lot easier than her starting cold turkey ... And I wouldn't have tried that before the study. It just didn't dawn on me that ... I didn't have any idea about that. The waiting ... I always thought that I waited but I never waited long enough. And so, watching [clinician] ... just watching her wait and me really waiting ... I've discovered that I just didn't wait long enough although I thought I was waiting long enough. That's made a real impression.

A staff member at an assisted living facility also recognized that the strategy of providing ample wait time was a helpful form of supported conversation. Additionally, she mentioned breaking things down, which seemed to refer to the supported conversation strategy of using appropriate closed and open-ended questions as well as clear, simple sentences. She also mentioned that interpreting gestures and establishing a routine were important facilitative strategies. She shared the following:

I think the study helped. It made a difference in techniques to get through to him. And learn to give him time to answer instead of just thinking, "Okay, you've had enough time, I'll try to answer for you." Just different ways of handling it and learning how to break things down and just trying figure out what topic he's on. And he's pretty good about gestures. So that helps a lot ... It just helps to know different techniques that you don't know in the beginning. Learning to give them time to answer is a whole different story. And then learning how to break things down and learning how to read their gestures. Let's see. Learning them themselves – learning their routines and what ticks them off really bad – learning not to do that.

The spouse of another person with aphasia also acknowledged the importance of wait time, which she referred to as patience. She reported that the strategies of providing verbal cues in the forms of cloze procedures and choice questions were helpful. Additionally, she shared the benefits of using humor in a helpful way.

Interviewer: Which strategy or technique do you think you use the most now?

Caregiver: As far as communicating with him? I think it's just, probably, just being patient. And if he tries to say something, I will ... and if I kind of know what he's trying to say ... if I say the first phrase or like a "Mmmm," you know, he'll go ahead and say it. And if I give him just little clues and hints, then he'll just put it together. And sometimes he'll say something and ... oh, this morning he was trying ... He wanted me to clean his glasses. And where this came from, I don't know, but he said, "Would you fix my radio?" and I "What?" [laughs] ... and he had pulled his glasses off so I knew what he wanted because he was handing them to me. And he stopped for a minute and I said, "Now what is that in you hand?" and he said, "Well, it's not my radio!"

Interviewer: So he knew what he had said and he knew that it was wrong?

Caregiver: Yeah. That it was wrong. Yeah. And he does that. It's like, "Ump. Nope." and I said, "Well, what is it then? Do you want me to clean ... ?" And he said, "My glasses."

Interviewer: So he completed the sentence?

Caregiver: Yeah. If I give him ... because I knew what he was wanting because the gesture was there. He took his glasses off and handed them to me. "Would you fix my radio?" Well, immediately he knew – no, that's not my radio. And I knew he wanted me to clean his glasses so, if I just said, "Clean ..." he picked up "My glasses."

In this particular research project, the AAC intervention involved a variety of facilitative communication techniques. The caregivers and PWA were not required to use the SGD device each time they conversed. Rather, the SGD was turned on and placed within reach of the PWA during each structured conversation that was observed. Thus, the PWA and their caregivers had access to the device if they desired to use it; however, they were not required or prompted by the clinician to do so.

Interestingly, the caregivers in this particular study reported that the SGD was a useful and helpful tool; however, they reported that they and their partners with aphasia rarely used the device outside of the intervention setting. Instead, some of the supported conversation techniques that had been trained were used more often. Overall themes identified from the interview transcripts included puzzlement (on the part of the caregivers) as to why the SGD was not used more often and possible reasons for its lack of use, including insufficient messages programmed/stored in the device, complexity of the SGD, time required to use the SGD, and preference for other modes of communication on the part of the user. Lack of knowledge, training, and/or practice with the SGD was not mentioned as a possible reason for lack of SGD use, which is also an interesting finding.

One caregiver provided two possible reasons for this lack-of-use phenomenon:

1. The SGD does not contain sufficient messages, especially novel message vocabulary, and/or the information is cumbersome to access.
2. The PWA prefers to use other modes of communication (e.g., speech and gestures) instead of the SGD. An excerpt of a dialogue between the interviewer and the caregiver is provided below.

Caregiver: [PWA] doesn't ... I don't know, I'm not really sure why we don't use it. She doesn't remember for one thing. And then, another, when we're talking about something, it's not on the computer. We put really basic information into her computer like a little bit about me, a little about the dogs, and a little bit about where she wants to eat. And pretty much, if I ask her. Like yesterday, I told her she was in charge of supper. And so, we were going to go out to eat and she needed to tell me where she wanted to go. Around six I asked her if she knew where she wanted to go and she said, "Yes, Jason's Deli." And it is on the computer, but she also ... She can kind of tell me verbally sometimes where she wants to do things ... Jumbo Joe's is the new hamburger place ... and she came up with that, too.

Interviewer: And she says it verbally?

Caregiver: Uh-hum, she says it verbally instead of ... I think it's a little faster she thinks, but I have never really asked her. She doesn't get out the computer and open up all the screens and stuff.

Another caregiver believed that the SGD would be a helpful device for the PWA to use with people who are unfamiliar, but that the PWA did not use it regularly with her. An excerpt of the interview transcript follows:

Caregiver: If he will pull it out ... well, it's sitting out anyway. It's always plugged up, ready to go, but if he ... once he gets into what he's wanting, it would help tremendously. There would be no questions as to what he's wanting or if he's needing anything, you know.

Interviewer: What sort of things are programmed in there that you'd think would help if he'd use it?

Caregiver: I think everything is programmed in there that would help him. Everything from his needs and wants to his personal, to his family, to his church, to places he's been, to his schooling, to ... he's got a lot of programs in there. It's very detailed as to what he might want to say ... politics; he's got that in there.

Interviewer: Does he know how to use it?

Caregiver: Yes.

Interviewer: Do you have a theory on why he doesn't use it?

Caregiver: I think he would just rather just get it figured out and get it over with. You know, just ...

Interviewer: Does it take a long time to where he'd not be able to use it ...

Caregiver: Not really. For the most part it doesn't. No, it would be very easy for him.

Interviewer: That's part of the study: Figuring out how valuable it is and if it would be used and if it is not used, why isn't it used?

Caregiver: I think, when it came down to it, if we had new people ... if we needed to, you know, if they didn't learn his routine very fast, it would be really beneficial to us for him to go to the computer and show ... because he can read it, and he can go to whatever he wants ...

> Interviewer: Does he then mostly try to communicate with you verbally?
> Caregiver: Yes.

Another caregiver shared that the SGD was a helpful tool for personal practice on the part of the PWA; however, it was not used frequently for interaction between the two of them unless she (the caregiver) prompted its use. She identified the computer's limited messages, level of complication, and time requirements as possible reasons for this lack of use during conversation. An excerpt is provided below.

> Interviewer: Does he really use it to communicate with somebody else?
> Caregiver: Uh ... not so much. I think he uses it more for his own information. You know. And I think he likes to put things in it and then, when the computer says what he's put into it, then he can repeat it, you know. So, I think he uses it more for himself than he does for actually communicating. You know, unless there's something he just really can't get over to ... you know, especially to me ... if he's trying to tell me something I'll go get it and I'll say, "Okay. Find something on there. A word. A picture. Anything." And he can do that. And sometimes that helps.
> Interviewer: So it's programmed adequately to be able to do that?
> Caregiver: Uh-huh. I think so. As far as just ... like in a conversation or something ... I think a lot of the times it may be something that just ... that he can't say that comes up only that one time, so that's not programmed, you know, into it. I mean, what's programmed into it are specific things. It's not like something that just might accidentally come up in a conversation, you know, and it would be impossible to get everything like that into it. So ... but it's helpful as far as, just like I say, words and pictures or if he can find something related to what he's trying to say, then it helps ... We've got a couple of different little programs in there that kind of simplify a lot of it. But, you know, if you're trying to find something to say, it's ... you have to go through too many different pages and too many different things trying to find what you're trying to say.
> Interviewer: You can lose the thought by the time you found it?

Caregiver: [laugh] Yeah. Yeah. By the time you find it, it's like, I don't remember now! But I think mostly it's just ... his patience isn't very long anymore. He gets real frustrated real easily if he has to go through too much trouble. He just won't do it. He'll say, "Oh forget it." So, we have simplified it as far as the program ... just certain programs ... as far as his basic needs and personal things ... you know ... that works out fine, but I don't know that he would ever really use it in a complete conversation.

A literature review regarding AAC and aphasia completed by Kraat (1990) noted that PWA "did not think to turn to use these alternative forms [of communication], could not shift strategies to use them, or somehow could not integrate them into real communication contexts" (p. 324). Although AAC options have increased and technology has advanced during recent decades, many of the inherent problems for SGD use by PWA continue. Garrett and Kimelman (2005) asserted that, PWA "will ultimately teach clinicians what works, and clinicians must continue to observe and listen to their individual successes to construct a more comprehensive and logical intervention philosophy for AAC and aphasia in general" (p. 369).

Qualitative analyses of interview transcripts provide valuable information regarding whether or not certain intervention strategies are socially valid to those directly and indirectly involved in their use (stakeholders). Although the Zens (2005) study did not include structured interviews with PWA, future studies should certainly attempt this. Schlosser (2003) stated that it is important to ask the people who experienced the treatment/intervention about the acceptability of the treatment. Because of the nature of chronic, severe aphasia, such interviews will be challenging; however, the information that could be potentially gained is critical for intervention planning as well as social validation purposes.

SUMMARY

Using conversation analysis as a tool for measuring the success of communication steps away from traditional approaches (e.g., standardized tests) and moves toward the goal of facilitating communication in functional contexts. Although conversation analysis has been employed as a means of determining communication success, it has not been employed as a tool for evaluating conversation in conjunction with AAC intervention using a customized SGD. The example studies mentioned in this chapter were attempts to evaluate conversations that are conducted using AAC systems, specifically SGDs.

The use of questionnaires and rating scales will continue to be important forms of social validation. A variety of measures (with strong construct validity) across different stakeholders should be used. Although statistically significant differences before and after AAC intervention using a SGD on social validity measures were not observed in the Ribitzki (2003) study, data indicated a trend toward improvement as a result of SGD intervention. Thus, further studies, perhaps using different measures (e.g., recently developed quality of life scales) and/or a greater number of participants, should be conducted before any definitive conclusions can be reached.

Qualitative analyses of interview transcripts provide information and insight that may not otherwise be gleaned in research studies. The field will benefit from increased use of interview analysis methodologies with several different stakeholders involved in the intervention process.

By observing, surveying, and interviewing the actual persons who participated in intervention, stakeholders can begin to better understand feelings, perspectives, and opinions, which can serve to better inform professionals who design and implement treatment protocols for the aphasia/ caregiver population. Laub and Sampson (2004) explained that quantitative findings can be enhanced by analyzing the qualitative data in relation to the quantitative results, thereby hopefully revealing some of the complex processes involved. Both sets of findings can provide valuable information toward improving intervention strategies, which is the ultimate goal.

When dealing with the challenging enigma of aphasia, direct, indirect, immediate community, and extended community stakeholders are all important in the social context of ensuring successful communication. AAC techniques can and should be evaluated using a variety of measures to determine their social validity, including conversation analysis, rating scales, and interviews. One can only begin to understand how another person feels about a particular intervention by carefully observing, asking, and listening to him/her. Once socially valid techniques have been identified, the ultimate goal of successful communication can be more easily met.

REFERENCES

American Speech-Language-Hearing Association (ASHA) (Producer). (1998). *ASHA telephone seminar: 'Treating aphasia outside the clinic'* [Motion picture]. Available from the American Speech-Language-Hearing Association, 10801 Rockville Pike, Rockville, MD 2085.

Beck, A. R., & Fritz, H. (1998). Can people who have aphasia learn iconic codes?. *Augmentative and Alternative Communication, 14*, 184–196.

Boles, L. (1998). Conversational discourse analysis as a method for evaluating progress in aphasia: A case report. *Journal of Communication Disorders, 31*, 261–274.

Bond, A., & Lader, M. (1974). The use of analogue scales in rating subjective feelings. *British Journal of Medical Psychology, 47*, 211–218.

Collins, S. L., Moore, R. A., & McQuay, H. J. (1997). The visual analogue pain intensity scale: What is moderate pain in millimetres?. *Pain, 72*, 95–97.

Damico, J., Oelschlaeger, M., & Simmons-Mackie, N. (1999). Qualitative methods in aphasia research: Conversation analysis. *Aphasiology, 13*, 667–679.

Engell, B., Hutter, B. O., Willmes, K., & Huber, W. (2003). Quality of life in aphasia: Validation of a pictorial self-rating procedure. *Aphasiology, 17*, 383–396.

Ferraz, M., Quaresma, M., Aquino, L., Atra, E., Tugwell, P., & Goldmith, C. (1990). Reliability of pain scales in the assessment of literate and illiterate patients with rheumatoid arthritis. *Journal of Rheumatology, 17*, 1022–1024.

Florance, C. (1981). Methods of communication analysis used in family interaction therapy. *Clinical Aphasiology, 11*, 204–211.

Freyd, M. (1923). The graphic rating scale. *Journal of Educational Psychology, 14*, 83–102.

Gainotti, G., Silveri, M. C., & Sena, E. (1989). Pictorial memory in patients with right, left and diffuse brain damage. *Journal of Neurolinguistics, 4*, 479–495.

Garrett, K., & Lasker, J. (2005). Adults with severe aphasia. In: D. R. Beukelman & P. Mirenda (Eds.), *Augmentative and alternative communication: Supporting children and adults with complex communication needs* (3rd ed., pp. 467–516). Baltimore: Brookes Publishing Co.

Garrett, K. L., & Kimelman, M. D. Z. (2005). AAC and aphasia: Cognitive-linguistic considerations. In: D. R. Beukelman, K. M. Yorkston & J. Reichle (Eds.), *Augmentative and alternative communication for adults with acquired neurologic disorders* (pp. 339–374). Baltimore, MD: Paul H. Brookes.

Goldstein, L. H., Canavan, A. G. M., & Polkey, C. E. (1988). Verbal and abstract designs paired associate learning after unilateral temporal lobectomy. *Cortex, 24*, 41–52.

Goodwin, C. (1995). Co-constructing meaning in conversations with an aphasic man. *Research in Language and Social Interaction 28*, 233–260.

Harms-Ringdahl, K., Carlsson, A. M., Ekholm, J., Raustorp, A., Svensson, T., & Hans-Goran, T. (1986). Pain assessment with different intensity scales in response to loading of joint structures. *Pain, 27*, 401–411.

Hayes, M. H. S., & Patterson, D. G. (1921). Experimental development of the graphic rating method. *Psychological Bulletin, 18*, 98–99.

Kagan, A. (1995). Revealing the competence of aphasic adults through conversation: A challenge to health professionals. *Topics in Stroke Rehabilitation, 2*, 15–28.

Kagan, A. (1998). Supported conversation for adults with aphasia: Methods and resources for training conversation partners. *Aphasiology, 12*, 816–830.

Kagan, A., Simmons-Mackie, N., Victor, J. C., Carling-Rowland, A., Hoch, J., Huijbregts, ... Mok, A. (2010). *Assessment for living with aphasia (ALA)*. Toronto, ON, Canada: Aphasia Institute.

Kagan, A., Winckel, J., Shumway, E., & the Aphasia Centre (Producers). (1996). *Supported conversation for aphasic adults* [Motion picture]. Pat Arato Aphasia Centre, Toronto, Canada.

Kelley, M., Heffer, R., Gresham, F., & Elliot, S. (1989). Development of a modified treatment evaluation inventory. *Journal of Psychopathology and Behavioral Assessment, 11,* 235–247.

Kendall, J., Hatton, D., Beckett, A., & Leo, M. (2003). Children's accounts of attention-deficit/hyperactivity disorder. *Advances in Nursing Science, 26,* 114–130.

Koul, R., & Corwin, M. (2003). Efficacy of augmentative and alternative communication intervention in individuals with chronic severe aphasia. In: R. W. Schlosser (Ed.), *The Efficacy of augmentative and alternative communication: Toward evidence-based practice* (pp. 449–470). New York: Academic Press.

Koul, R., & Harding, R. (1998). Identification and production of graphic symbols by individuals with aphasia: Efficacy of a software application. *Augmentative and Alternative Communication, 14,* 11–23.

Koul, R., & Lloyd, L. L. (1998). Comparison of graphic symbol learning in individuals with aphasia and right hemisphere brain damage. *Brain and Language, 62,* 398–421.

Koul, R. K., Corwin, M., & Hayes, S. (2005). Production of graphic symbol sentences by individuals with aphasia: Efficacy of a computer-based augmentative and alternative communication intervention. *Brain and Language, 92,* 58–77.

Kraat, A. (1990). Augmentative and alternative communication: Does it have a future in aphasia rehabilitation? *Aphasiology, 4,* 321–338.

Lasker, J. P., Garrett, K. L., & Fox, L. E. (2007). Severe aphasia. In: D. R. Beukelman, K. L. Garrett & K. M. Yorkston (Eds.), *Augmentative communication strategies for adults with acute or chronic medical conditions* (pp. 163–206). Baltimore, MD: Paul H. Brookes.

Laub, J. H., & Sampson, R. J. (2004). Strategies for bridging the quantitative and qualitative divide: Studying crime over the life course. *Research in Human Development, 1,* 81–99.

Light, J. (1989). Toward a definition of communicative competence for individuals using augmentative and alternative communication systems. *Augmentative and Alternative Communication, 5,* 137–144.

Lomas, J., Pickard, L., Bester, S., Elbard, H., Finlayson, A., & Zoghaib, C. (1989). The communicative effectiveness index: Development and psychometric evaluation of a functional communication measure for adult aphasia. *Journal of Speech and Hearing Disorders, 54,* 113–124.

Lyon, J. G., Cariski, D., Keisler, L., Rosenbek, J., Levine, R., Kumpula, J., … Blanc, M., et al. (1997). Communication partners: Enhancing participation in life and communication for adults with aphasia in natural settings. *Aphasiology, 11,* 693–708.

Manochiopinig, S., Sheard, C., & Reed, V. A. (1992). Pragmatic assessment in adult aphasia: A clinical review. *Aphasiology, 6,* 519–533.

McCall, D., Shelton, J. R., Weinrich, M., & Cox, D. (2000). The utility of computerized visual communication for improving natural language in chronic global aphasia: Implications for approaches to treatment in global aphasia. *Aphasiology, 14,* 795–826.

Murray, L. L., & Chapey, R. (2001). Assessment of language disorders in adults. In: R. Chapey (Ed.), *Language intervention strategies in aphasia and related neurogenic communication disorders* (4th ed., pp. 55–126). Baltimore: Lippincott Williams & Wilkins.

Oelschlaeger, M., & Thorne, J. (1999). Application of the Correct Information Unit analysis to the naturally occurring conversation of a person with aphasia. *Journal of Speech, Language, and Hearing Research, 42,* 636–648.

Paul, D. R., Frattali, C. M., Holland, A. L., Thompson, C. K., Caperton, C. J., & Slater, S. C. (2004). *Quality of communication life scale (ASHA QCL).* Rockville, MD: ASHA Publications.

Price, D., McGrath, P., Rafii, A., & Buckingham, B. (1983). The validation of visual analogue scales as ratio scale measures for chronic and experimental pain. *Pain, 17,* 45–56.

Ribitzki, T. (2003). *Efficacy of computer-based voice output communication intervention in persons with chronic severe aphasia.* Unpublished master thesis. Texas Tech University Health Sciences Center, Lubbock, TX.

Schlosser, R. W. (2003). In: *The efficacy of augmentative and alternative communication* (pp. 203–228). London, UK: Academic Press.

Shelton, J., Weinrich, M., McCall, D., & Cox, D. (1996). Differentiating globally aphasic patients: Data from in-depth language assessments and production training using C-VIC. *Aphasiology, 10,* 319–342.

Simmons-Mackie, N. (2008). Social approaches to aphasia intervention. In: R. Chapey (Ed.), *Language intervention strategies in aphasia and related neurogenic communication disorders* (5th ed., pp. 290–318). Baltimore: Lippincott Williams & Wilkins.

Soh, G., & Ang, H. G. (1992). Comparison of two pain rating scales among Chinese cancer patients. *Chinese Medical Journal, 105,* 953–956.

Wapner, W., & Gardner, H. (1981). Profiles of symbol-reading skills in organic patients. *Brain and Language, 12,* 303–312.

Zens, C. (2005). *Effects of caregiver training and AAC intervention on facilitating communication skills of individuals with aphasia.* Unpublished master thesis. Texas Tech University Health Sciences Center, Lubbock, TX.

CHAPTER 9

THE PROCESS OF EVIDENCE-BASED PRACTICE: INFORMING AAC CLINICAL DECISIONS FOR PERSONS WITH APHASIA

Rajinder Koul and Melinda Corwin

INTRODUCTION

It is critical for effective clinical practice, as well as public policy, that sound efficacy data are available on augmentative and alternative communication (AAC) intervention with persons with aphasia. With the advent of evidence-based practice (EBP) in health care, funding agencies are increasingly requiring data that demonstrate interventions actually work. Schlosser and Raghavendra (2003) define EBP in AAC as "the integration of best and current research evidence with clinical/educational expertise and relevant stakeholders perspectives, in order to facilitate decisions about assessment and intervention that are deemed effective and efficient for a given direct stakeholder" (p.3). The purpose of this chapter is to apply concepts presented in previous chapters to clinical contexts and to further examine the data on the efficacy of AAC intervention for persons with aphasia using an EBP process as proposed by Schlosser and Raghavendra (2003). It is important to consider evidence from the available research when selecting an AAC intervention approach for an individual with chronic severe

Augmentative and Alternative Communication for Adults with Aphasia
Augmentative and Alternative Communications Perspectives, Volume 3, 155–164
ISSN: 2047-0991/doi:10.1108/S2047-0991(2011)0000003015

aphasia. The integration of the best research evidence with clinical expertise and the perspectives of stakeholders is the key to bridge the gap between research and clinical practice.

AAC INTERVENTION WITH APHASIA: AN EBP ILLUSTRATION

While working with a client who has chronic severe Broca's aphasia in our clinic, we applied the seven steps identified by Schlosser and Raghavendra (2003) to illustrate the use of EBP for AAC intervention with persons with aphasia. These steps are described below.

Step 1: Asking a Well-Built Question

The first step in the EBP process is the formulation of a well-built question that can enable a systematic search of the available evidence so that clinically relevant answers can be found (Schlosser, Koul, & Costello, 2007). A case report followed by the EBP question is listed below.

Clara is a 65 year-old woman who sustained a left hemisphere stroke (anterior middle cerebral artery distribution) 4 years ago, resulting in chronic severe Broca's aphasia and apraxia of speech. Associated impairments included right hemiplegia that caused her to use a wheelchair. At the time of her stroke, Clara had recently retired from operating a clothing store. She had been widowed for 3 years and was living in her home independently. Following her stroke and subsequent hospitalization, she returned to her home, and her daughter and son-in-law moved in with her. She received speech-language treatment through a home health agency for 5 months. Treatment techniques included melodic intonation therapy and mapping therapy (Helm-Estabrooks & Albert, 2004; Thompson, 2001). She now communicates through pointing, gestures, and head movements accompanied by speech output in the form of "yes" and "no." Most other verbalization attempts result in perseveration of approximation of her daughter's name (i.e., "Sarah Sarah Sarah") rather than the target word. She typically makes her basic wants and needs known to her son-in-law and daughter using the previously mentioned nonverbal communication strategies; although, her daughter expressed that they often "have to play 20 questions" before arriving at Clara's actual thought/request. Clara enjoys playing card games and has friends over approximately once every couple of months for a "game night." Her daughter would like her to be able to express her needs, wants, and thoughts more clearly/efficiently with both familiar and unfamiliar communication partners. Clara would like to fly to visit her son who lives out-of-state, but she has expressed concern due to her lack of ability to communicate with others (e.g., flight attendants, cab drivers). To prepare Clara to communicate more effectively in her home and community settings, we considered aided AAC intervention.

Specifically, we asked the following question: Should we introduce Clara to a technology based AAC intervention approach (e.g., a speech generating device (SGD) as a part of a treatment package) or a no-technology based AAC intervention approach (e.g., a communication book as a part of a treatment package)?

Steps 2 and 3: Selecting Evidence Sources and Executing the Search Strategy

Studies comparing the efficacy of technology-based AAC intervention approaches to no-technology AAC intervention approaches in persons with chronic severe Broca's aphasia across experimental and non-experimental settings would be ideal. However, our search strategies revealed no published studies that compared the relative effectiveness of two or more treatment approaches in the area of aphasia and AAC. Thus, we searched for similar or related studies. The search methods for this systematic review included searching electronic and bibliographic data-bases, hand searches of selected journals in the areas of AAC and aphasia, as well as ancestry searches. We primarily relied on this systematic review and other narrative reviews (Beukelman, Fager, Ball, & Dietz, 2007; Koul & Corwin, 2003; Lasker, Garrett, & Fox, 2007; van de Sandt-Koenderman, 2004) in addition to publications in refereed journals to answer our clinical question.

Step 4: Examining the Evidence

We evaluated the evidence for technology based and no-technology based AAC intervention approaches by appraising the methodological quality of each study on several distinct dimensions (Schlosser & Wendt, 2006). As stated in Chapter 4, the evaluation criteria for single subject design studies included (1) experimental control demonstrated within a single participant and across different participants, (2) operationally defined independent and dependent variables to allow for replication, and (3) reported inter-observer agreement and treatment integrity data that were appropriate. Evaluation criteria for group design studies included the following: (1) threats to internal validity were satisfactorily ruled out, (2) data were analyzed using appropriate statistical techniques and allowed effect size to be determined, and (3) a control condition and/or a control group was included. Our findings are summarized in the following paragraphs.

Technology-Based AAC Intervention Approaches
With the rapid proliferation of computer technology in the past decade, AAC aids such as SGDs and software programs for hand-held multipurpose electronic devices (e.g., iPod, iPad) have become increasingly available to persons with aphasia (Koul & Corwin, 2011; Koul, Petroi, & Schlosser, 2010). Most dedicated SGDs, software programs, and applications (e.g., DynaVox V™ & Vmax™ by DynaVox®, SpeechPRO software by Gus Communications Inc., SmallTalk by Lingraphica® Company and Vanguard Plus by PRC) are not disorder specific. These devices/software programs are designed and promoted to be used by persons with speech and language impairments, regardless of the cause of the impairment. However, there is one commercially available SGD (i.e., Lingraphica® by Lingraphica®: The Aphasia Company™) that is specifically designed and promoted for use by individuals with aphasia.

Efficacy of Technology-Based AAC Intervention Approaches
Studies involving technology-based AAC intervention with individuals with chronic severe Broca's aphasia have indicated that these individuals are able to access, identify, select, and combine graphic symbols to produce simple phrases and sentences (Koul, Corwin, & Hayes, 2005; Koul, Corwin, Nigam, & Oetzel, 2008; Koul & Harding, 1998; McKelvey, Dietz, Hux, Weissling, & Beukelman, 2007; Rostron, Ward, & Plant, 1996). Further- more, to get a greater insight into individual study outcomes, we used the criteria proposed by Rispoli, Machalicek, and Lang (2010) with minor modifications to classify methodologically sound AAC intervention studies that incorporated technology as part of the treatment package into studies with positive, negative, and mixed outcomes. Studies in which the data indicated that the dependent measures improved for all participants were classified as studies with positive outcomes. Negative outcomes referred to studies in which the data indicated that the dependent measures did not change as a result of AAC intervention, and studies in which at least half of the participants demonstrated improvement in all the dependent measures targeted were classified as studies with mixed outcomes. Using the aforementioned criteria, we classified five single subject design studies and two group design studies as having positive outcomes for persons with chronic Broca's aphasia (Beck & Fritz, 1998; Koul & Harding, 1998; Koul et al., 2005, 2008; McKelvey et al., 2007; van de Sandt-Koenderman, Wiegers, & Hardy, 2005). There were no studies that met Schlosser and Wendt's (2006) methodological appraisal criteria that were classified as having either negative or mixed outcomes. However, despite positive

outcomes, the variability of results within and across studies and lack of treatment generalization data are indicative of the critical need for additional research using well controlled experimental designs. It is important that future research endeavors focus on collecting outcome data on AAC interventions using designs that rule out concerns related to internal and external validity.

No-Technology AAC Intervention Approaches
No-technology-based intervention approaches do not involve the production of speech output upon selection of a message. Communication books/boards, cue cards, and memory books are examples of no-technology approaches. Garrett and Lasker (2005) and Lasker et al. (2007) proposed an intervention approach that focuses on the communication needs, cognitive-linguistic competencies, and participation levels of persons with aphasia. This approach proposes that both technology-based and no-technology-based approaches can be used as part of a multimodal treatment package to facilitate communication in persons with aphasia.

Efficacy of No-Technology-Based AAC Intervention Approaches
A number of studies have been conducted in which AAC intervention involved the use of alphabet cards, photographs, graphic symbols, written choices, gestures, drawing, writing, communication boards, or remnant books (Fox, Sohlberg, & Fried-Oken, 2001; Ho, Weiss, Garrett & Lloyd, 2005; Lasker, Hux, Garrett, Moncrief, & Eischeid, 1997; Ward-Lonergan & Nicholas, 1995). A review of these studies indicates that people with Broca's aphasia are able to use various no-technology options with varying degrees of success. Furthermore, few studies that met our methodological criteria had positive outcomes (e.g., Garrett, Beukelman, & Low-Morrow, 1989; Ho et al., 2005). However, the preponderance of case studies in existing no-technology-based AAC intervention literature reduces the strength of the evidence that indicates positive or mixed outcomes. Case studies by their very nature can neither rule out internal validity nor provide external validity.

Summary of the Evidence
The purpose of this chapter was to find out whether sufficient data are available to answer questions about the efficacy of AAC intervention in people with aphasia. The answer to that question is as follows: First, data on the efficacy of AAC intervention for persons with aphasia indicate that both technology-based and no-technology-based AAC options are effective to varying degrees in changing the dependent variables under study in

experimental contexts (Fox et al., 2001; Garrett & Lasker, 2005; Koul et al., 2005, 2008, 2010; Koul & Harding, 1998; Lasker et al., 2007; McKelvey et al., 2007; van de Sandt-Koenderman et al., 2005). Second, despite limited controlled data, Koul et al. (2010) reported several studies that provide conclusive, preponderant, and suggestive evidence in support of the use of AAC methods with persons with aphasia (e.g., Beck and Fritz, 1998; Koul et al., 2005, 2008; Koul & Harding, 1998; McKelvey et al., 2007).

Step 5: Applying the Evidence

Results indicated that at least in the experimental context, both technology-based and no-technology-based AAC intervention options appeared to be effective. Although there are several studies that provide conclusive and preponderant evidence as to the efficacy of AAC intervention in persons with aphasia, the variability within and across studies and the lack of data regarding generalization reduces the enthusiasm for that evidence. Thus, either option appeared to be a viable one. It was then time to discuss the findings with the relevant stakeholders, in this case Clara and her primary communication partners. We considered their viewpoints, preferences, concerns, and expectations when making the decision regarding which AAC intervention to try. In this case, Clara and her adult daughter and son-in-law indicated that they were interested in trying a technology-based AAC intervention approach, specifically an SGD. Clara indicated that she wanted to be able to express her thoughts and be heard. Her daughter expressed that she thought Clara's friends and family members, as well as members of the community at large, would be more receptive to spoken words than printed words or pictures.

Step 6: Evaluating the Evidence Application

Once the decision was made to try an SGD, an assessment and implementation protocol was developed that included participation of both the direct stakeholder (Clara) as well as her primary communication (i.e., daughter and son-in-law). A predictive assessment that involved matching the capabilities of Clara using several criterion referenced tasks was used to select an SGD that best met her communication needs and goals (Glennen, 1997). Clara was given an opportunity to try several different SGDs from our AAC laboratory over a period of six weeks, and an SGD was selected that best fit her capabilities and was desired by her. Following this trial period, we prepared an assessment report for Medicare funding for the SGD that documented her communication impairment, sensory skills, cognitive skills, and language skills, as well as her ability to access the device using a touch screen. This report also summarized her daily communication needs and communication goals. Additionally, we borrowed the recommended SGD from our AAC laboratory and started implementing an AAC intervention program that included training Clara on specific techniques and strategies, which increased her ability to share information with others. With input from Clara and her family and friends, we programmed easily accessible messages in her device so that she can continue to maintain interactions with her friends and acquaintances. We also trained her primary communication partners (i.e., daughter and son-in-law) using Kagan's (1995) partner-dependent approach. This approach involves training/teaching communication partners skills so that they can in turn reveal the communicative competence of the person with aphasia. Our intervention program also measured the frequency of the use of her SGD outside the clinical context by checking the log files in the device and the effectiveness of her communication by administering the communicative effectiveness index (CETI) scale (Lomas et al., 1989) to her daughter and son-in-law. This scale measures the effectiveness of functional communication of the persons with aphasia as reported by the caregiver.

Step 7: Disseminating the Findings

The final step in the EBP process involves disseminating our experiences and outcomes at professional conferences and in journals so that we all can learn from the information and further our awareness regarding future research that is needed in this area. We are in the process of submitting a manuscript based on data collected with Clara and other persons with aphasia regarding the efficacy and social validity of AAC intervention that includes SGDs as part of the treatment package.

CONCLUSIONS

To adequately support persons with aphasia in maximizing their full inclusion, social integration, employment, and independent living, it is critical to know which interventions work and which interventions work better than others. However, the serious paucity of controlled data prevents us from doing so. Future research efforts must focus on going beyond case studies to research that uses controlled designs to evaluate effects of treatment. We may be able to bridge the gap between research and clinical practice by obtaining evidence that is devoid of methodological concerns and can be generalized to a target population.

ACKNOWLEDGMENTS

Portions of this chapter were based on an article: Koul, R. K. & Corwin, M. (2011). *Augmentative and alternative communication intervention for persons with chronic severe aphasia: Bringing research to practice.* Manuscript submitted for publication.

REFERENCES

Beck, A. R., & Fritz, H. (1998). Can individuals who have aphasia learn iconic codes? *Augmentative and Alternative Communication, 14*, 184–196.

Beukelman, D. R., Fager, S., Ball, L., & Dietz, A. (2007). AAC for adults with acquired neurological conditions. *Augmentative and Alternative Communication, 23*, 230–242.

Fox, L. E., Sohlberg, M. M., & Fried-Oken, M. (2001). Effects of conversational topic choice on outcomes of augmentative communication intervention for adults with aphasia. *Aphasiology, 15*, 171–200.

Garrett, K., & Lasker, J. (2005). Adults with severe aphasia. In: D. Beukelman & P. Mirenda (Eds.), *Augmentative and alternative communication* (3rd ed., pp. 467–504). Baltimore, MD: Paul H. Brookes.

Garrett, K. L., Beukelman, D. R., & Low-Morrow, D. (1989). A comprehensive augmentative communication system for an adult with Broca's aphasia. *Augmentative and Alternative Communication, 5*, 55–61.

Glennen, S. (1997). Augmentative and alternative communication assessment strategies. In: S. L. Glennen & D. C. DeCoste (Eds.), *Handbook of augmentative and alternative communication* (pp. 149–192). San Diego, CA: Singular.

Helm-Estabrooks, N., & Albert, M. L. (2004). *Manual of aphasia and aphasia therapy* (2nd ed.). Austin, TX: PRO-ED.

Ho, K. M., Weiss, S. J., Garrett, K., & Lloyd, L. L. (2005). The effect of remnant and pictographic books on the communicative interaction of individuals with global aphasia. *Augmentative and Alternative Communication, 21*, 218–232.

Kagan, A. (1995). Revealing the competence of aphasic adults through conversation: A challenge to health professionals. *Topics in Stroke Rehabilitation, 2*, 15–28.

Koul, R. K., & Corwin, M. (2003). Efficacy of AAC intervention in individuals with chronic severe aphasia. In: R. W. Schlosser (Ed.), *The efficacy of augmentative and alternative communication: Toward evidence-based practice* (pp. 449–470). San Diego, CA: Academic Press.

Koul, R. K., & Corwin, M. (2011). *Augmentative and alternative communication intervention for persons with chronic severe aphasia: Bringing research to practice.* Manuscript in submission.

Koul, R. K., Corwin, M., & Hayes, S. (2005). Production of graphic symbol sentences by individuals with aphasia: Efficacy of a computer-based augmentative and alternative communication intervention. *Brain and Language, 92,* 58–77.

Koul, R. K., Corwin, M., Nigam, R., & Oetzel, S. (2008). Training individuals with severe Broca's aphasia to produce sentences using graphic symbols: Implications for AAC intervention. *Journal of Assistive Technologies, 2,* 23–34.

Koul, R. K., & Harding, R. (1998). Identification and production of graphic symbols by individuals with aphasia: Efficacy of a software application. *Augmentative and Alternative Communication, 14,* 11–23.

Koul, R. K., Petroi, D., & Schlosser, R. (2010). Systematic review of speech generating devices. In: S. Stern & J. Mullennix (Eds.), *Computer synthesized speech technologies: Tools for aiding impairment.* Hershey, PA: IGI Global.

Lasker, J., Garrett, K. L., & Fox, L. E. (2007). Severe aphasia. In: D. Beukelman, K. Garrett & K. Yorkston (Eds.), *Augmentative communication strategies for adults with acute or chronic medical conditions* (pp. 163–206). Baltimore, MD: Paul H. Brookes.

Lasker, J., Hux, K., Garrett, K., Moncrief, E., & Eischeid, T. (1997). Variations on the written choice communication strategy for individuals with severe aphasia. *Augmentative and Alternative Communication, 13,* 108–116.

Lomas, J., Pickard, L., Bester, S., Elbard, H., Finlayson, A., & Zoghaib, C. (1989). The communicative effectiveness index: Development and psychometric evaluation of a functional communication measure for adult aphasia. *Journal of Speech and Hearing Disorders, 54,* 113–124.

McKelvey, M., Dietz, A., Hux, K., Weissling, K., & Beukelman, D. (2007). Performance of a person with chronic aphasia using scene display. *Journal of Medical Speech Language Pathology, 15,* 305–317.

Rispoli, M., Machalicek, W., & Lang, R. (2010). Subject review: Communication interventions for individuals with acquired brain injury. *Developmental Neurorehabilitation, 13,* 141–151.

Rostron, A., Ward, S., & Plant, R. (1996). Computerized augmentative communication devices for people with dysphasia: Design and evaluation. *European Journal of Disorders of Communication, 31,* 11–30.

Schlosser, R. W., Koul, R., & Costello, J. (2007). Asking well-built questions for evidence-based practice in augmentative and alternative communication. *Journal of Communication Disorders, 40,* 225–238.

Schlosser, R. W., & Raghavendra, P. (2003). Toward evidence-based practice in AAC. In: R. W. Schlosser (Ed.), *The efficacy of augmentative and alternative communication: Toward evidence-based practice* (pp. 259–297). San Diego, CA: Academic Press.

Schlosser, R. W., & Wendt (2006). *The effects of AAC intervention on speech production in autism: A coding manual and form.* Unpublished manuscript, Northeastern University, Boston.

Thompson, C. (2001). Treatment of underlying forms: A linguistic specific approach for sentence production deficits in agrammatic aphasia. In: R. Chapey (Ed.), *Language intervention strategies in aphasia and related neurogenic communication disorders* (4th ed., pp. 605–628). Baltimore, MD: Lippincott Williams & Wilkins.

van de Sandt-Koenderman, M. W. (2004). High tech AAC and aphasia: Widening horizons? *Aphasiology, 18*(3), 245–263.

van de Sandt-Koenderman, M., Wiegers, J., & Hardy, P. (2005). A computerized communication aid for people with aphasia. *Disability and Rehabilitation, 27*, 529–533.

Ward-Lonergan, J. M., & Nicholas, M. (1995). Drawing to communicate: A case report of an adult with global aphasia. *European Journal of Disorders of Communication, 30*, 475–491.

ABOUT THE EDITOR

Rajinder Koul holds a PhD in Speech-Language Pathology with an emphasis in augmentative and alternative communication (AAC) from Purdue University. He is currently a professor and chair in the Department of Speech, Language, and Hearing Sciences at Texas Tech University Health Sciences Center and associate dean for Research for the School of Allied Health Sciences. He has published in peer-reviewed journals such as *Brain and Language, Augmentative and Alternative Communication, Journal of Speech, Language, and Hearing Research, Acta Neuropsychologica, American Journal of Speech-Language Pathology: A Journal of Clinical Practice, Journal of Assistive Technologies,* and *Disability and Rehabilitation.* He is the recipient of the Mary E. Switzer Distinguished Rehabilitation Research Fellowship from the National Institute on Disability and Rehabilitation Research, United States Department of Education. In 2005, he was named a Fellow of the American Speech, Language and Hearing Association (ASHA). The status of Fellow is one of the highest honors ASHA can bestow.

AUTHOR INDEX

Lapointe, L. L., 30, 115, 122
Lasker, J. P., 48, 53–54, 56–60, 79–80,
    85, 87, 93–95, 121, 141, 157,
    159–160
Laub, J. H., 151
Laures, J., 8
Leo, M., 143
Leonard, C., 122
Levine, R., 131, 139
Light, J., 119, 123, 131
Lloyd, L. L., 36, 48, 52, 88–89, 96, 138,
    159
Logemann, J., 11
Lomas, J., 76, 117, 130, 138–139, 161
Lorenzen, B., 8
Love, R. J., 20
Low-Morrow, D., 88, 159
Lowell, S., 32
Lu, A., 39
Lustig, A. P., 122
Lyon, J. G., 37, 39, 117, 131, 139
Lytton, R., 36

Machalicek, W., 71, 158
Mahendra, N., 7, 27
Manasse, N., 93
Mancinelli, J. M., 10
Manders, E. E., 123
Manochiopinig, S., 130
Marien, P., 22
Marshall, R. C., 32
Martin, N., 34
Martino, R., 11
Massaro, M., 122
Matchar, D. B., 8
Matson, J. L., 118
Mayer, J. F., 8
McCall, D., 96–97, 104–105, 111, 141
McCoach, D. B., 117
McGrath, P., 138

McHugh, R. E., 32
McKelvey, M. L., 51–52, 68, 72, 74, 96,
    109, 158, 160
McNeil, M. R., 22, 95–96
McQuay, H. J., 138
Mesulam, M. M., 22, 23
Miller, N., 10
Mirenda, P., 36, 49–51, 94, 97
Mok, A., 138
Moncrief, E. M., 53, 85, 87, 121, 159
Moore, R. A., 138
Mountcastle, V. B., 48
Munoz, M., 39
Murray, L. L., 8, 24, 38, 96, 100, 130
Musson, N., 27
Myers, J. L., 34
Myers, P. S., 12

Naeser, M. A., 16
Newhoff, M., 8, 96
Nicholas, M., 53, 69, 72, 74, 85, 89, 159
Nigam, R., 49, 50, 72, 158, 160
Nishikawa, L. K., 88
Njardvik, U., 117

Obler, L. K., 18
O'Connor, B., 18
Odell, K. H., 8
Oelschlaeger, M., 133
Oetzel, S., 49–50, 72, 158, 160
Ogletree, B. T., 86, 96, 120, 124

Page, J. L., 32
Paghera, B., 22
Palumbo, C. L., 16
Patterson, D. G., 138
Patterson, J. P., 39, 40
Patterson, K. E., 33
Paul, D. R., 76, 138
Perecman, E., 95

SUBJECT INDEX